Zalman & Leah:
    I hope th.. ✓ W9-DEW-416
you great joy — and to
Cleveland. Come visit.
                    All The Best
                        A.

From
FEAR
to
ETERNITY

From Fear To Eternity
10 Steps to Achieving the Benefits of Being Jewish
By A. Lefkowitz

First Printing July 2002

Copyright © 2002 Andrew R. Lefkowitz

Library of Congress Cataloging-in-Publication Data
For Library of Congress information, please contact the publisher.

Lefkowitz, A.

From Fear To Eternity : 10 Steps to Achieving the Benefits
of Being Jewish / By A. Lefkowitz

ISBN: 1-931681-23-6

Published by:
Heights Press
P.O. Box 21647
Cleveland, Ohio 44121-0647

Distributed by:
Israel Book Shop
501 Prospect Street, Suite 97
Lakewood, New Jersey 08701
Tel: 732. 901.3009 / Fax: 732. 901.4012
Email: isrbkshp@aol.com

Designed, produced and printed by:
Bottom Line Design
718.377.4567
www.bottomlinedesign.com

Table of Contents

Three Important Milestones

From
FEAR
to
ETERNITY

*10 Steps to Achieving
the Benefits of
Being Jewish*

A. Lefkowitz

Dedication

This book is dedicated to the memory of:

Joan Lefkowitz

A Great Friend—who could never do enough for others, and made everyone feel better about themselves.

A Second Mom—to those who lost a parent at an early age, as she did, and to many others whom she instinctively knew needed a hug or a shoulder to lean on.

A True Professional—who was a mentor and role model to countless of her co-workers.

An Optimistic—no matter what challenge she faced, her optimism never wavered—and that optimism rubbed off on all who were fortunate enough to know her.

She Possessed True Wisdom—the wisdom of a bygone era that came from the heart, as well as from the head.

She Epitomized The Trait of Empathy—she defined and exuded "class" by always putting others first, not just sometimes, but all the time.

She Was Unfailingly Devoted To Her Family—she strengthened her husband, children and grandchildren through constant encouragement. She was the first to show a family picture to a new acquaintance and the last to want to leave a family gathering. And above all, she never felt she had done enough, when in reality she had always done more than any one could expect.

Only now can we truly appreciate the void that her passing has left in the lives of her family and friends.

May the mitzvahs engendered by this book be a source of endless merit for her.

Acknowledgements

Acknowledgements in books like this one can either start or end with thanking the One Above. I prefer to start that way, because everything I have flows from His benevolence. I will mention only one specific note of thanks among the many that come to mind, and that is that He never gave up on me. No matter how far I have strayed, He continues to welcome me back.

My parents, Henry and Joan Lefkowitz have always lived by the famous adage known as the Golden Rule, and have tried their best to teach their children to do the same. They raised us in a warm and supportive atmosphere. They allowed us to reach for the stars without having to worry about who would catch us if we fell short. Their home was, and continues to be, a Jewish home, in which people from disparate backgrounds have always felt comfortable. Their approach to Judaism instilled in me an open-mindedness that fostered my recent growth. They are models of how parents, friends and spouses should treat one another. May we all be blessed to realize the incredibly positive impact they have had on their children, grandchildren and the community in which they live.

My Rebbe, Rabbi Yisroel Brog has sacrificed much to help me and his many other students. Almost every word in this book is based on something I heard from Rabbi Brog. I am extraordinarily grateful to him for sharing his wisdom and insights with me. I owe him a debt that I shall never be able to repay. If you were to ask me to describe what Rabbi Brog means to me and his other students, I would respond the way Rabbi Simcha Wasserman responded when asked to describe his father, the great Rabbi Elchonon Wasserman. I would be silent for a few minutes, and would then tell you that words cannot describe what he has done for us. That no string of adjectives could properly convey the commitment he has made to my family and me. May I and his other students be blessed to continue to have him as our *Rebbe.*

Rabbi Chaim Feld and Rabbi Yehuda Appel of Aish HaTorah in Cleveland each spent countless hours teaching me the basics and counseling me on a variety of difficult subjects.

Words cannot describe the debt of gratitude that I owe to Rebbetzin Chassie Brog, my *rebbe's* wife. She made me feel as comfortable in her home as I am in my own. The Brog children have always been similarly gracious. Always supportive. Never judgmental. Uniformly willing to sacrifice their beds, time with their parents and anything else they possess for those of us who are less fortunate than they are. The apple surely does not fall far from the tree.

No grandparent ever treated a grandchild with more love than I was treated by Rebbetzin Rochel Sorotzkin and Rabbi and Rebbetzin Shmuel Brog, my *rebbe's* mother-in-law and parents, respectively. When I meet one of their descendents, I feel as though we are related. May the entire Brog and Sorotzkin families be blessed with joy.

In the course of my journey, I spent 12 months living near Telshe Yeshiva, a Jewish center for learning on 55 pristine acres outside of Cleveland, Ohio. Telshe has been one of the world's great houses of Jewish scholarship for over 100 years. Because of their level of brilliance and achievement, you would expect that the Telzers would be a bit aloof. And they would certainly have the right to be so. Nothing could be farther from the truth. In over six years of being associated with literally hundreds of Telzers, I have only heard words of acceptance and encouragement. I was only made to feel embarrassed by the hundreds of invitations I received for *Shabbos* and holiday meals.

I would like to thank the leaders of Telshe Yeshiva for their individual acts of kindness and for collectively establishing an institution in which beginners are treated so graciously.

It is impossible to thank everyone at Telshe Yeshiva who went out of his or her way to assist me. My special friends at Telshe who are a great source of inspiration to me are Rabbi and Rebbetzin Yitzchok Sorotzkin, Rabbi and Rebbetzin Zalman Gifter, Rabbi and Rebbetzin Yecheskal Munk, Rabbi and Rebbetzin Yankel Katz, Rabbi Yossi Sova, Rabbi Eli Skorski, Rebbetzin Sorah Eta Katz and Dr. and Mrs. Yonason Fisgus. And a special thanks to all of the members of the Telshe Kollel who were magnanimous in their support.   .

I would like to thank Rabbi Yitzchok Scheinerman. Everyone should have a study partner who has his knowledge, experience, sense of humor and, especially when it come to me, patience.

From the bottom of my heart I would like to thank Moshe Weizner. A Holocaust survivor. A hero. I true friend who

I had the honor of praying with, and learning from, for three years.

Rabbi Brog's students all go out of their way to help one another. The assistance I received, and the friendships I have made, could fill another book.

I spent 18 glorious days at Yeshiva Ohr Somayach in Jerusalem. Each of the rabbis I learned with was incredibly dedicated to bringing Torah to the students who were fortunate enough to attend classes there.

A number of people read this manuscript before it was a book. Rabbi Moshe Garfunkel, Rabbi Ephraim Nisenbaum and Rabbi Sholom Shapiro sacrificed valuable time from their teaching and learning to help me. Lisa Farmer and Chaya Newman provided valuable insights and many corrections to my grammar, spelling and punctuation. I don't believe I'd have finished this book without a lot encouragement. They may be surprised to see their names here, but Rabbi Paysach Krohn, Rabbi Nosson Scherman, Ron Gluck and Yosef Zuckerman each offered kind and encouraging words of support that each came at a time when I wasn't sure I'd be able to finalize this project.

Publishing a book is a true team effort. I would like to thank Moshe Kaufman at Israel Book Shop for taking a chance and working so diligently to distribute this manuscript, Mrs. Elky Langer for her keen eye and Yitzchok Saftlas at Bottom Line Design for his creative inspiration.

It takes a *shtetl* to raise a *ba'al teshuva*—to bring someone to Torah observance. Among those who went out of their way to help me were; Jacob Kovel, Fred Schwartz, Dr. Rodney

Green, Alan Polster, Dr. Michael Harris and, in general, the observant community of Cleveland, Ohio which combines the *menchlakeit* of *Yiddishkeit* and Midwest graciousness. Rhonda and Bobby Sigman plucked me out of oblivion and welcomed me into their home for countless Torah classes that served as the foundation for a wonderful friendship. Rabbi Chaim Zwick is a childhood friend who introduced me to Rabbi Brog and whose entire family continues to be intertwined with mine on a constant basis. Mrs. Susan Sokol operates Simcha Link, a wonderful service in Chicago that introduced me to my wife, and has performed the same service for countless others. I won't ever forget the valuable time Gidon Shoshan spent learning with me.

I would also like to thank my many friends who have taken a sincere interest in my journey, who have been support-ive and continue to involve me and my family in their joyous family events.

My siblings have been with me through thick and thin. I feel so blessed to have my sister Nancy and brother James so closely involved in my life on every level. My in-laws Seymour and Sara Reichbart enrich my life and the lives of my wife and children more than they will ever know.

To describe my life partner as a "wife" is like describing Sandy Koufax as a "pitcher." She is a fantastic mother to our children. A short order cook and an executive chef. She is a chauffer and teacher. A nurse and personal shopper. She is a handyman and travel agent. An accountant and referee. She performs all of these functions, and more, so that I may learn, pray, write and earn a living with a clear mind. She especially performs these functions so that when I am home

I can devote myself to our children. May she be blessed to continue to receive Yiddish *nachas* from our children and from me. May we be blessed to be together in all of our endeavors for many years to come.

Introduction

When I started investigating an observant lifestyle, I had the same questions that most people have. How can a book, the Torah, written over 3,000 years ago, be relevant to me today? How can the Torah be interpreted to prohibit me from driving a car on *Shabbos*? How can the Torah prohibit me from eating pork now that we have modern packaging techniques and the Food and Drug Administration to protect us? And all the structure! Do this. Don't do that.

In fact, what I learned was that living according to the Torah is the only way to maximize the many pleasures of being Jewish, and for that matter, the day-to-day pleasures of life in general.

As I progressed in my studies, I tried to tell others about what I was going through, and I had a typical result—something that has happened to all of us. We tell a story to a friend that we think is absolutely hilarious, and are met with a blank stare. And how do we always respond? "You had to be there." When I tried to explain to my friends and family how there is so much joy, so much fulfillment, so much meaning that is available to any of us who become more observant, I was met with a blank stare. When I described how family life is enriched and personal achievement is given a perspective that is unheard of outside of the observant community, I was again met with a blank stare. And how did I respond? "You have to be there." You have to check it out for yourself.

Essentially, this book is my attempt to record, in a question-and-answer format, the basic tenets of Judaism as they have recently been explained to me. These basic tenets are quite different from the A, B, C's of Judaism that I was exposed to as a child. Thus, at first, I tended to dismiss them as irrelevant. And it's easy to see why.

Because our society's laws define our rights, not our obligations, we aren't comfortable being told what foods we should eat or how often we should pray. Because we were taught that doing what makes us feel good is the key to our happiness, we don't want to feel imposed upon. Because we were taught that the future holds the key to our happiness, we don't seriously examine exactly where we are today and how we got there. Most of us don't feel obligated, or even interested, in examining what it means to be Jewish, except in a very superficial manner.

The good news is that when we finally do confront the reality of our existence as Jews, it makes going forward that much easier.

There is a man by the name of Uri Zohar who was at one time the most famous entertainer in all of Israel. I have been told that he was David Letterman, Frank Sinatra and Robin Williams all rolled into one. He had it all. But he abandoned his star-studded life and dedicated himself to Torah observance. Rabbi Zohar has written a book. Its title, *My Friends, We Were Robbed*, sums up my feelings about those of us who grew up without the benefits of an observant lifestyle.

We may have been robbed, but we can retrieve what was taken from us. It isn't easy, and it doesn't happen overnight. But we can do it. We can all do it.

About the Writing

I have symbolically chosen A. Lefkowitz as the author. I have always gone by Andy, except for about a week during law school when I used Andrew, the name on my birth certificate. As I have become more and more observant I have tried to evolve into being Avi, which is short for Avraham, which is the Hebrew name I was given at my *bris*.

This book is essentially a conversation between Andy and Avraham. It is the questions that Andy, or any Jew raised to call himself reform, conservative or secular, would ask a friend or relative who decided to become more observant.

You will note many words that are written in italics. These words are Yiddish or Hebrew terms, such as *shul* for synagogue, *brachos* for blessings, and so on. Using these terms help impart a certain flavor to the Avraham end of the conversation, so I have included them here. To make the meaning as clear as possible, all italicized words are explained the first time they are used and are also included in the glossary at the end of the book.

Another convention I have followed is that of hyphenating the word "G-d," or using the term *Hashem* (literally meaning "the name," which also refers to G-d), to signify respect for the name of G-d.

Disclaimer

I'm sure you're familiar with the disclaimer, "The views expressed by the hosts are not necessarily those of the management." This book is exactly the opposite. Except where I have referred to personal experiences, "The views expressed herein are my humble attempt to record those views which are *solely* those of the management"—that is, Torah scholars. *Any mistakes or errors in expressing those views are completely my fault, and I humbly ask for your and their forgiveness.*

Why Me?

I thought of calling this book, "Why Me?" Really, why should I be one of the few non-observant Jews who traveled down the road toward an observant lifestyle? There is nothing in my background that would lead anyone to think that I was a likely candidate. I was not one of those tortured souls who was forever searching for greater meaning in life.* See Below

I grew up in the suburbs of Cleveland, Ohio. Throughout high school I defined myself as a jock, with a major in basketball. I went to college at Miami University in Oxford, Ohio, where I majored in accounting. I snuck into law school at Case Western Reserve University and somehow ended up near the top of my class after the all-important first year, and on law review. After graduating, I moved to ocean front apartments, first in Venice Beach and then Santa Monica, California, where I worked for the Los Angeles office of a Wall Street law firm. I moved to Dallas and then to Miami, where I lived on a private island for four years. I traveled throughout Europe and South America and took at least ten trips to Caribbean Islands. I spent close to a month in Australia. Ultimately, I was the youngest partner at one of Wall Street's largest law firms, then left to start a

---

*In the movie *The Elephant Man*, a terribly disfigured man exclaims; "I am not an animal!" I think there is a tendency to think that anyone who would give up a secular life for an observant lifestyle is a loser or a nerd or is otherwise looking for a crutch. I added the paragraph about my personal life instead of screaming: "I am not a loser" because a number of people who read the book thought that it was important that you understand that my choice to become more observant was just that—a choice.

business that was dangerously close to being wildly successful, but wasn't.

Basically, I liked my life. I had ups and downs, both personally and professionally, but I always thought tomorrow was going to be a better day.

Such was the case when I awoke one beautiful tropical morning about six years ago in my home in Coconut Grove, Florida. As I packed for a long weekend in Cleveland, Ohio where I would be visiting my parents, I caught the over-zealous warnings of the local weatherman about a "tropical depression." Like most people who have lived in South Florida for more than a few years, I did not take these warnings very seriously, because they are inevitably false alarms.

When the cab driver arrived to take me to the airport, I was, as usual, behind schedule. As I rushed out of my house, I noticed that I hadn't pulled my car into the garage the night before. Since I was already late, I decided another few days in the Florida sun wouldn't do it too much damage. Little did I know.

My trip to Cleveland generated the usual feelings of anticipation about seeing my parents and the few close friends with whom I had stayed in contact during the twelve years I'd been gone. But I knew it was just a visit. What could be more important than waking up to the warm breezes that blew through the tropical village in which I lived? What could compare to attending the gala openings of new restaurants, bars and galleries that dominated Miami's nightlife?

After collecting my luggage, my father and I drove to the

home in which my parents have lived for the last quarter of a century. In Cleveland, people actually listen to weather broadcasts because the temperature can change dramatically in a short amount of time. So I wasn't surprised when my dad told me that the "tropical depression" that was threatening Miami had been upgraded to a "hurricane watch." I, of course, waved it off.

The next day, the "hurricane watch" was upgraded to a "hurricane warning" and people began to evacuate. I thought of catching a flight back to Miami, but decided against it. Instead, I sat and waited and watched CNN. I woke up the next morning to find that Hurricane Andrew had turned the neighborhood I lived in upside down and inside out.

I prayed more in the days following Hurricane Andrew's arrival in Miami than the previous 36 years combined. Until I could determine that all of my friends had survived the worst natural disaster in the history of the United States, I did not have a moment's peace. I was also more than a little curious to know how much damage had been done to my house (not much) and to my car that I had left outside (a lot). Once I had made those determinations, I went back to being blissfully devoid of any spiritual thought or commitment.

Little did I realize that my namesake would not just transform the landscape of South Florida, but also the landscape of the rest of my life.

I stayed in Cleveland for the next month waiting for electricity, telephone service and water to be restored to my home in Miami. Even though I had been away for twelve years, I realized that I had some decent business opportunities if I could spend time in the Cleveland area. When I returned to Florida, my intention was to work one week a month in Cleveland and three weeks a month in Florida.

After a few months of going back and forth between Cleveland and Miami, I decided to make a permanent move to Cleveland. Although being close to my parents was a factor in my decision, I had no objective reason for making the move. There just seemed to be some force that was pulling me back to the city where I grew up. To say that my friends in Florida thought I was crazy to move from sunny Miami to overcast Cleveland would be an understatement. But somehow, I knew I was making the right decision.

About two weeks after I had moved back to Cleveland, I was having dinner with a friend from law school. A high school friend of his approached us and asked me to come to his house on Sunday morning to learn with an orthodox rabbi. When I finished laughing, I said "No" or perhaps it was "Are you kidding?" A week later I was in the same restaurant with my same friend and the same friend of his came up to us, this time with his wife. Again he asked me if I would like to learn with an orthodox rabbi. I didn't laugh quite so hard this time, and politely told him that if I woke up early enough I'd stop by.

Why did I even consider his offer? I had never even met an orthodox rabbi. In fact, I don't think I had ever met a conservative rabbi, at least not on purpose. My exposure to the rabbinate for the previous 25 years had been limited to weddings and bar mitzvahs officiated by reform rabbis.

At that point in my life I was not exactly an early riser, especially on weekends. But that Sunday I was up with the roosters. When I arrived at the home of the couple who were hosting the class, I inquired when the rest of the students would be arriving. I was told, "There aren't any other students." I was thinking of a polite way to extricate myself from what I thought would be an extremely uncomfortable situation when the rabbi walked in.

He was a couple of years younger than me, but had a definite bearing of confidence well beyond his years. He also had an overpowering enthusiasm for life that was apparent the moment we were introduced. We chatted for a few minutes and played enough Jewish geography to establish a link between us. We then sat down to "learn."

The class was entitled "The Five Levels of Pleasure." After a few introductory remarks, he explained, "There is a hierarchy of pleasure in this world based on the Torah." I felt my eyes getting a little watery. He went on, "To experience the highest levels of pleasure, you have to become a connoisseur of pleasure, and the only way to do that is by studying the Torah." My eyes filled with tears. He continued, "The only way to obtain the maximum amount of pleasure in this world is through living according to the Torah." By now, tears were streaming down my face.

I found myself crying in front of strangers, over a topic I knew nothing about: the Torah. I mean, I knew the name, but I couldn't quite put my finger on its significance. Yet the mere mention of the Torah was sending uncontrollable waves of emotion through me, the likes of which I had never felt before.

The more I learned about Judaism, the more I wanted to know. I began to observe a few laws related to *kashrut* and felt pretty good about myself for having done so. Then I started to lose momentum. I mentioned this to a rabbi I had been studying with. He suggested that I contact a Rabbi Brog, who he thought could get me back on track. Another rabbi also mentioned the name of Rabbi Brog, and that he was associated with something called Telshe Yeshiva. I had lived in Cleveland for over twenty-five years and had never heard of Telshe Yeshiva, which is like saying you live in Boston and have never heard of Harvard. Anyway, a childhood friend of mine called one day and said he wanted me to meet his *rebbe*, who happened to be the same Rabbi Brog I had been hearing so much about.

It was impossible for me to ignore three people telling me that I should meet Rabbi Yisroel Brog. Important events, which I knew weren't coincidences, had taken place over the past two years, and had re-shaped the quality and direction of my entire life. So I went to meet him.

We sat at his dining room table, and once again the words of a rabbi moved me to tears. I don't remember what we talked about, but my life hasn't been the same since. This book will surely testify to that.

Someone who read a draft of this book commented that I should explain why I had been moved to tears that Sunday morning when I heard my first class on the Torah, and again when I met Rabbi Brog. Was it because I felt I had discovered a sense of belonging? Did I unexpectedly realize a longing for a more meaningful existence? Were my emotions intensified by the manner in which the messenger delivered his message? The answer to all of these questions is *yes.* But still I ask, *"Why me?"*

Our tradition is that we all get a wake-up call, or a series of calls. You may not be brought to tears as I was, but sooner or later you will have to make a decision: whether to continue the status quo, or to explore the benefits of becoming more observant.

To make an efficient decision between two courses of action, we need to know the ramifications of our choices. What we will be getting, and what we will be giving up? If you aren't observant, you already know the benefits, and the drawbacks, of a secular lifestyle. To know if we are making the right decision about our religious observance, it would follow that we should explore what our lives would be like if we were to live according to the Torah.

I hope this book will give you a glimpse of the benefits of being observant, and what you may encounter along the way.

From FEAR to ETERNITY

Step One

Get Into
the Zone

Step 1: Get into the Zone

Our family sport is basketball. My father played in the NBA; my brother made the team at a Big Ten school as a walk-on; and two of my uncles played college ball. When I was in high school, I thought of little else. I remember one game against Twinsburg, our archrival, when I was in *the zone.* The basket seemed to be twice its normal size. I couldn't wait to get my hands on the ball. No matter how off balance I was when I shot, the ball kept going in. To get to that point, I had devoted thousands of hours to dribbling and shooting a basketball. And then the game was over. But I will never forget that feeling of being in *the zone.*

I Get The Same Feeling When I Play Golf.

I know. There is a point when the club hits the ball perfectly. There's a magical feeling that runs through your hands, up your arms and into your shoulders. You can tell by the sound of the impact, without looking, that the ball went exactly where you wanted it to go. The problem is, that feeling only occurs on a golf course, only lasts for a moment and is purely physical.

So How Do I Recapture That Magical Feeling Without A Golf Club?

By learning Torah. It may not happen the first time you go to a class or pick up a Jewish *sefer* (book), but eventually it will send shivers up and down your spine. It will touch your spirit in a way that a golf game never could.

Learning Torah Puts You In The Zone?

Like you wouldn't believe. Many people can get that feeling just by listening to a class. Of course, the more one learns, the easier it is to get into *the zone*. For instance, learned Jews get into *the zone* any time they want by discussing a passage in the *Gemara*, the commentary on the earliest codification of Jewish oral law. It's exciting to watch them discuss an issue that seems to have no practical ramifications. They can be in *the zone* for hours at a time and do it day after day, year after year. Even a great golfer will tell you he only hits a couple of great shots a round. Once you master the basic skills of studying Torah, you can access the feeling of hitting a hole-in-one as often as you want.

So Where Do I Start?

Classes. Just about every large city has outreach organizations which offer classes on a variety of subjects. Many *shuls* (synagogue) also sponsor classes. Try different classes/rabbis until you find one approach that feels comfortable, and then go religiously. There are two basic approaches to going to classes. The first, which is the way we all start, is by being a Torah Tourist. We check things out, absorb some basic information and take a few mental pictures. Later, when we find the right approach and rabbi to convey it, we really start to learn—by internalizing the information and allowing it to change us.

What About Reading Some Books? I Can Use My Lunch Hour

That's a great start. However, our sages teach us that the best way to learn is with a study partner. A certain amount of review by yourself is helpful, but you have to find some-one who will set aside time to learn with you on a regular basis. I was extremely embarrassed when I started doing this because the person I was paired up with was about half my age. But like most learned Jews who are given the op-portunity to help someone like me, he never once made me feel that it was anything but his privilege to be help-ing me. I persisted and he persisted. I still have a long way to go, but I now possess a few of the basic tools that are needed to learn *Gemara*.

What Should I Do Until I Can Get A Study Partner?

Pick up the Stone Edition of the Chumash, the first five books of the Torah. The first five books of the Torah, called the *Chumash*, are divided into chapters, called *parshas*, which are read weekly on *Shabbos* (Sabbath), so the entire *Chumash* is read throughout each year. It doesn't matter where you are in the world, if you walk into a *shul* on *Shabbos*, they will be reading the exact same *parsha*. So, start by reading the weekly *parsha* in English. Try to come up with some questions. Then read it again with the footnotes.

I Was Thinking Of Going To A Class On Kaballah.

I'm not sure you're quite ready. Although the study of *Kaballah*—Jewish mysticism—has become quite popular with Jews who want to feel good about their Jewishness, it's not recommended for beginners. I think it has some-thing to do with the fact that although *Kaballah* is intellectually and spiritually stimulating, it does not require us to change the way we act. Accordingly, it doesn't help most of us to maximize the benefits of being Jewish. The general rule seems to be that one shouldn't study *Kaballah* until the age of 40. Of course, that presupposes that one has been learning Torah his entire life and has a substantial understanding of Jewish law and observance.

So What Should I Study When I'm Not Learning Torah?

Everyone is different. I happen to enjoy reading inspirational stories. Go into any Jewish bookstore. You will find hundreds of books about Jewish heroes.

My must-read list of inspirational stories includes:

1. *Lieutenant Birnbaum*
   (Mayer Birnbaum, Mesorah Publications)

2. All For the Boss
   (Ruchama Shain, Feldheim Publishers)

3. Each volume of *Visions of Greatness*, especially the story on page 90 of Volume II
   (Rabbi Yosef Weiss, CIS Publishers)

4. All of the *Maggid* books
   (Rabbi Paysach Krohn, Mesorah Publications)

5. *They Called Him Mike*
   (Yonason Rosenblum, Mesorah Publications)

6. *The Committed Life*
   (Rebbitzen E. Jungries)

7. *A Tzaddik in Our Time*
   (Simcha Raz, Feldheim Publishers)

8. *The Other Side of the Story*
   (Rebbetzin Y. Samet, Mesorah Publications)

9. *Rabbi Chaim Gelb: A Lifetime of Chesed*
   (Rabbi David Fisher, Mesorah Publications)

10. *Above the Bottom Line*
    (Hanoch Teller)

What About Books Written For People Like Me Who Are Trying To Find Out What It Means To Be More Observant?

I'd suggest:

1. *Choose Life* (Rabbi E. Tauber)

2. *My Friends, We Were Robbed* (Uri Zohar)

3. *Anatomy of a Search* (Rabbi Akiva Tatz)

4. *Rejoice O Youth* (Rabbi Avigdor Miller)

5. *To Become One* (Rabbi E. Tauber)

6. *From Central Park To Sinai*
   (Roy S. Neuberger, Jonathan David Publishers)

What About Books That Will Help Me Learn Basic Halacha—Jewish Laws?

My friend Shmuel suggests:

1. *The Laws of B'rachos* (blessings)
   (Rabbi Binyamin Forst, Mesorah Publications)

2. *The Shabbos Home*
   (Rabbi Simcha Bunim Cohen, Mesorah Publications)

3. *The Shabbos Kitchen*
   (Rabbi Simcha Bunim Cohen, Mesorah Publications)

Any Other Books I Should Pick Up?

I would be remiss if I didn't recommend:

1. *The Pirkei Avos Treasury* (coffee table size book with green cover from Mesorah Publications)

2. Any books by or about the Chofetz Chaim, including but not limited to, *A Lesson A Day*

3. Any book by Aryeh Kaplan

Anything Else?

Need you ask? Get a subscription to the *Yated, Hamodia, and/or The Jewish Observer*. They offer insights into the *parsha*, reporting of events in Israel, the US and the rest of the world, biographies of our most heroic figures, and much, much more. It's also interesting to scan their advertisement to see what goods and services are available in the observant community.

I Hate To Ask, But Are There Other Educational Opportunities Available For Someone Like Me?

Of course, why do you think they call us the People Of The:

Cassette. There are thousands of tapes available on any number of topics. Rabbi Avigdor Miller has over 6,000 tapes available.

Telephone. There are numbers you can call 24 hours a day to hear classes on hundreds of different topics. Ask your rabbi for a recommendation.

This All Sounds Great, But I Can Barely Read Hebrew.

I know the feeling. For the first two years that I was attending Torah classes, I limited myself to learning in English. One of my rabbis repeatedly warned me, "Andy, you're going to have to learn Hebrew if you want to grow." He should have added: "You're going to be sorry for waiting so long," because I am. There is no way of getting around it. You have to break your teeth and learn Hebrew.

I Have To Break My Teeth?

Only figuratively. Even if you have a hard time with languages as I do, there is a sense of déjà vu in studying Hebrew. Notwithstanding that sense of recognition, learning to read Hebrew as an adult is not an easy task for some of us. Learning it well enough to understand the prayers we say every day is even harder. For men, the ultimate goal is to learn Hebrew well enough to study *Gemara* in the original text. There is a program for learning Hebrew based on the fact that over 75 percent of the Torah consists of less than 300 words. Recently, I have been able to do some one-on-one learning with a rabbi and with a *yeshiva* (Jewish high school/college) student, and that has been extremely helpful. But no matter what approach you take, it basically comes down to practice.... practice.... practice.

What If I'm Breaking My Teeth *But Not* Getting Into The Zone?

You mean what if it's all pain and no gain. There is no such thing as *no gain* when it comes to learning Torah. By just making the attempt to learn, you are establishing an incredible connection to *Hashem* (G-d). If you put in the effort, you will ultimately have a breakthrough. I am told it's guaranteed.

I'm Overwhelmed. How Do I Decide Which Class, Which Book and Which Tape? And In What Order?

See Step 2, "Find A Rabbi Who Will Be Your Rebbe"

Step Two

Find a Rabbi Who Will Be Your Rebbe

Step 2: Find A Rabbi Who Will Be Your Rebbe

I put on a little weight a few years ago and decided to start working out to get back in shape. Because I had always played a lot of sports, I decided I could develop my own exercise routine. For the first few weeks I was so sore I couldn't sleep more than a few hours each night. Then I settled into a pattern where some weeks I'd lose a few pounds, and some weeks I'd gain a few pounds. After a couple of months I was ready to give up.

I finally realized that I didn't know what I was doing and I hired a trainer. He analyzed my strengths and weaknesses. He showed me exactly how to do each exercise and in what order. He pushed me when my motivation waned and encouraged me when I was feeling low. I would never have reached my goals if I hadn't taken the advice of someone who knew more than I did.

So too a *rebbe*.

Don't You Mean A Rabbi?

No, a *rebbe* (rhymes with Entebbe). A rabbi is someone who typically teaches Torah to groups of people, either from a pulpit or in some type of classroom setting. He is also the person you may go to when you have questions about Jewish law. A *rebbe* is also involved in teaching Torah. The difference is that a *rebbe's* approach is personalized for each of his students. A *rebbe* personally molds and develops each of his students according to their particular strengths and weaknesses, so they can reach their full potential.

A Rebbe *Personalizes His Approach To Each Student?*

He has to. When we started, my *rebbe* focused on my need to feel that I would remain part of a community as I became observant. That I would still have friends and could be close to my family. With another student, my *rebbe* focused on his need to feel that his becoming observant was unique (which it was). With some students, he immediately has them learning extremely difficult concepts, while with others he concentrates on the beauty of *Shabbos*. The result is that we all felt comfortable in our surroundings and motivated to move forward. It takes someone who can analyze each student's needs and use distinct approaches to help each one achieve his goal.

I Went To High School. I Know What A Teacher Does.

There's a big difference between a *rebbe* and a teacher. A *rebbe's* guidance will benefit every facet of your life. Except in rare cases, the expertise of teachers lies in their ability to convey knowledge on one subject matter. If they teach science, they probably don't teach math or English. A teacher is not expected to develop a student's character traits or to impart his or her "self" into a student, whereas a *rebbe* does both. A *rebbe* will help you look at every facet of life from a Torah perspective. He will help you respond to everyday events and, most importantly, to life's more stressful situations, in the most efficient manner.

A *rebbe* will always possess wisdom and insight that you don't have. You can ultimately know more about math than a high school math teacher, or even a college math professor, if you dedicate yourself to learning that subject. It may even be possible to surpass your *rebbe* in pure Torah knowledge. But I don't know anyone with the type of *rebbe* that I do who would ever stop going to their *rebbe* for advice.

A *rebbe*'s greatest pleasure is your growth. The greatest pleasure a *rebbe* can have is when a student asks him a question he has to ponder, or better yet, research. A fundamental rule of learning Torah is questioning the person you are learning from. A *rebbe* doesn't want you to just accept information. He wants you to ask for more detail, for sources and for *Hashem's* rationale, if it's discernable. Most *rebbes* will attest that, "I have learned more from my students than anyone else," because of the questions they are required to answer.

You are building a relationship to last a lifetime. Generally, a student-teacher relationship lasts for a semester, or perhaps a few years. You may go back to visit on spring break, but after a few years even that casual contact usually stops. A relationship with a *rebbe* will last a lifetime. I used to learn with a doctor whose *rebbe* was once speaking in a city about five hours from where we live. He got out of work early, drove to hear his *rebbe*'s class, spoke to his *rebbe* for a few minutes and then drove home just in time to take a shower and go back to work. When I spoke to him later that day, he was on fire, even though he hadn't slept the night before. He hadn't learned with his *rebbe* on a full-time basis in over ten years, but they had maintained an unbelievably close relationship.

A Rebbe *Sounds Almost Like A Father.*

You're not the only one who thinks so. One of the To-rah giants of pre-war Europe, Rabbi Elchonon Bunim Wasserman, visited the United States in 1937 to raise funds for his *yeshiva*. He was scheduled to return to Poland af-ter the Nazis (may their names be erased) had conquered Czechoslovakia and Austria, just five months prior to the outbreak of World War II. When it was suggested that for the sake of his safety he should stay in the United States and send for his two sons, he responded, "I don't have only two sons; I have 400—the *yeshiva* students. How can I leave them?"

In the *Shema*, our most famous prayer, we find the admon-ishment: "...you shall teach your children." Our sages teach us that in this context, *children* is interpreted as *students*, to emphasize that a *rebbe's* obligation to educate his stu-dents is no less than the life-long responsibility a father has to educate his own children. Moreover, you will often find that *rebbes* and their students relate to each other in much the same way that a parent relates to a child.

Do Rebbes *Also Function As Rabbis?*

Of course. A rabbi is often associated with a pulpit or a congregation, where he may be a rabbi or teacher to large numbers of individuals. A rabbi is also someone we go to for answers on questions of Jewish law. Concurrently, he may be a *rebbe* to a limited number of individuals with whom he spends an exhaustive amount of time on a one-on-one basis.

Do I Really Need A Rebbe?

Yes. When the Sages of the *Mishna*, the earliest codification of Jewish oral law, instructed each Jew to "make himself a *rebbe*," nearly every father knew the Torah backwards and forwards and almost every *shul* doubled as a *yeshiva*. Even in that environment, our Sages recognized that each person needed a *rebbe* to help him grow to his full potential. How much more important is that directive today for those of us who grew up in secular homes, and are now trying to find our way! It's important to note that the obligation is on the student to make the effort to establish the *rebbe-talmid* relationship, not the other way around. Accordingly, if you think there is a rabbi who would be willing to become your *rebbe*, it is incumbent upon you to make the effort.

Are You Positive I Need A Rebbe?

Absolutely. Could you build a skyscraper without an architect? Could an army go into battle after reading a book on how to fight, but without a general to lead them? Well, maybe, but could you imagine the casualties! I wouldn't say that it's impossible to achieve the maximum benefits of being Jewish without the guidance of a *rebbe*, but the benefits of having one are immeasurable. From my perspective, chief among those benefits is being guided to use the little time we have effectively, and not making the more obvious mistakes that a *rebbe* would help you avoid. Although I have no way of knowing for sure, I would think that many people who had started the journey toward an observant lifestyle, and didn't make it all the way, would have succeeded if they had found a *rebbe*.

I Go To Classes ...

That's how I started ... but it's not enough. I started out by going to one class a week with my first *rebbe* and worked my way up to four classes a week over a two-year period.

Your First Rebbe?

It happens. There are many excellent organizations that specialize in laying the foundation that allows us to discover more about our religion. We often develop extremely close relationships with the rabbis and *rebbetzins*—a rabbi's wife—who run these organizations. If we are smart, we continue to stay close to them, even as we become involved with other rabbis as we evolve. Jews who are born into Torah observant homes often have a *rebbe* in elementary school, then one in junior high, another in high school, another at yeshiva and still another when they settle into a new community.

Do FFB's (Frum/Observant From Birth) Have Rebbes?

It's important for everyone. The advice of our Sages "to make yourself a *rebbe*" applies to all Jews, even FFB's. The one advantage many FFB's have is that they can make their father, or as stated above, their teachers, their *rebbe*, while those of us who have returned to an observant lifestyle must look elsewhere. From my limited experience, it seems that more often than not, observant FFB's have a *rebbe*. My *rebbe* certainly does.

Do Only Men Need Rebbes?

Of course not. Every benefit of having a *rebbe* applies equally to men and women. The ideal situation is for a man to have a *rebbe* and a woman to have a *rebbetzin* because of the nature of the relationship. However, many women have *rebbe's* because of geographic restraints, and certainly when it comes to asking questions regarding Jewish law.

You Were Talking About Taking Classes With Your First Rebbe.

Right. The classes were a wonderful way to gain background knowledge and insight into Judaism, but then I hit a wall. Fortunately, a childhood friend of mine came home from studying at a *yeshiva* in Israel and brought me to meet "his" *rebbe*. I sat with his *rebbe* in his dining room and we spoke for less than an hour. Although I can't relate his exact words, I immediately felt a special connection to him. I returned to learning on a regular basis, with the knowledge that I had found *my rebbe*.

What Made You Decide To Make That Particular Rabbi Your Rebbe?

Four factors come to mind. First, he was able to demonstrate how wisdom gleaned from the Torah could help me make better decisions in all phases of my life, including important relationships and my business. That is, he showed me how to get more out of the gifts *Hashem* had given me, but which I wasn't utilizing. Second, he was very reassuring about my ability to overcome the challenges that he knew lay ahead. Third, I was overwhelmed by the way each member of his family treated each other and everyone else they came into contact with—demonstrating heart-felt, genuine respect. Fourth, I found that I was inspired by the personalized approach to learning that he developed for me.

So How Do I Get A Rebbe?

Seek and ye shall find. A famous bank robber was once asked why he robbed banks. "Because that's where the money is," he replied. If you live in a city with a *yeshiva*, you could call the office and explain your interest. You could also just show up. Someone will surely ask you if they can be of service. Similarly, if you live in a city with a *kollel* (center for young married post-graduate Torah students), ask to speak to the *rosh* (head) of the *kollel*. Otherwise, try an orthodox *shul* or outreach organization. You could also contact the American Jewish Outreach Professionals for a recommendation. If you are still having trouble, drop me a line (See "Your Story") and I will ask my *rebbe* to make a suggestion. Also, it wouldn't hurt to spend a few moments praying for *Hashem* to send you your *rebbe*.

I'm Still Not Sure About How This Works In Real Life...

Don't worry, just keep on reading. There is a lot more to talk about related to the importance of having a *rebbe*, how to obtain one and how to maximize the relationship you will have with your *rebbe*. Those thoughts can be found under *Three Milestones—Your Rebbe*.

From FEAR to ETERNITY

Step Three

Hashem, Hashem, Hashem

Step 3: Hashem, Hashem, Hashem

O ne of my best friends is in the business of buying, managing and selling real estate. He lives, eats and breathes real estate. He can recite all sorts of complicated ways of analyzing the purchase or sale of real estate involving internal rate of return, capitalized costs, triple net rent and a hundred other terms and ratios. But he always says that there are really only three important factors in real estate: location, location, location.

So too with being Jewish. In analyzing "how Jewish we are," we can look at how we observe *Shabbos*, if we give more than our fair share to charity, how much respect we show our parents, and a myriad of other actions which we are obligated to perform or abstain from performing. But in the final analysis, it all comes down to our relationship with *Hashem, Hashem, Hashem*. What we have to ask ourselves is: "How much are we involved with *Hashem*, and to what extent are we really connecting ourselves to Him?"

Did You Believe in G-d Before You Started Learning With A Rabbi?

Not so you'd notice. Even though I "went to temple" as a child and had a bar mitzvah/bowling party, I had no strong belief in the existence of a Supreme Being. When I was a sophomore in high school, my grandmother, with whom I was extremely close, died very suddenly. I became an agnostic. I attributed my successes to my efforts, and my failures to the efforts of others.

How Long Did It Take You To Believe In G-d After You Started Learning?

I was very fortunate. On a very basic level, I felt some connection during my first class. It was about the five levels of pleasure that every Jew can experience and the "false pleasures" that bog us down. As a secular Jew, I was consumed with the "pursuit of happiness." The concept that I was missing out on entire categories of pleasure was quite disturbing to me. When I felt the tears rolling down my cheeks, I knew I was connecting to something extraordinary.

What Happened Next?

I felt cheated. I knew nothing about 3000 years of *Hashem* and the Torah guiding Jewish history. I didn't know that the Torah provides advice and counsel on how to make our day-to-day lives more fulfilling. Why hadn't anyone told me that our relationship with *Hashem* is not only based on belief or faith, but also on fact? As I looked back on what seemed at the time to be isolated and unrelated events, I could see a pattern which could only be explained by the fact that *Hashem* was involved in shaping my life.

What Does It Mean To You To Believe In G-d?

Developing a relationship based on love and fear. Loving *Hashem* is easy once one internalizes all of the blessings that He bestows upon each and every one of us every single day. The fear part is a little more difficult. For a long time I thought that fear of *Hashem* meant that we should fear the punishment that will be coming our way when we do something wrong. But *Hashem* doesn't punish us.

It Sure Seems That Way.

I used to feel that way, a lot. But consider this. If some-one stuck his finger in a light socket, would he complain that the electric company was punishing him because he got a shock? When we do things that are not in our best interest, there are consequences—not punishments. Accordingly, the fear we should develop is the understanding that by committing sins, we are distancing ourselves from *Hashem*, when our goal should be to get as close to Him as possible.

What Is The First Step To Believing In G-d?

It can start with just being aware of the world around us. When we look at a picnic table, we can deduce a number of facts. Someone cut down a tree, sawed it into planks and then nailed the planks together. Now, examine something as complicated as our eyes. They have auto focus, adjust to light and darkness, pick up every possible shade of every possible color and have a built-in lubricating device that never needs refilling. No camera comes close. Many scientists are now coming to the conclusion that something as basic as a molecule couldn't have occurred by chance. If one of the smallest, most basic forms of our existence can't be explained as having been randomly created, then it's clear that waterfalls, snow-capped mountains and sunsets are not just happenstance.

It Would Help If G-d Communicated With Me Directly.

He does. In three ways. Think of *Hashem* as the Chief Executive Officer of the world, and we as His employees.

The CEO of a company communicates with His employees in three ways. He speaks to them, he writes them memos and he has an executive staff meet with them on a face-to-face basis. Similarly, *Hashem* spoke to us at Mt. Sinai, He wrote us a memo on company policy (the Torah) and he has assigned rabbis to meet with us on a face-to-face basis.

Do You Have Any Concrete Facts And Figures That Support The Fact That G-d Wrote The Torah?

Get ye to Discovery. The Discovery Program, which is operated by Aish Hatorah and other outreach organizations, proves that Hashem exists and that He wrote the Torah—so many different proofs, in fact, that it's almost impossible to come to any other conclusion. I say almost impossible, because if someone attends a Discovery Program with absolutely no background and a negative view of religion, prejudice and ignorance can combine to block the message. Otherwise, the proofs that are presented are irrefutable. My favorite has to do with the fact that the Torah states two conditions for an animal to be kosher: it must have split hooves and chew its cud. That is, all animals with both of those characteristics are kosher, and all animals with only one, or neither, of these characteristics are not kosher. Although there are many animals with neither of these characteristics, the Torah lists by name the only four animals that would ever exist in the history of the world with only one of those characteristics. The Torah was written over 3,000 years ago. If the author of the Torah wasn't an all-knowing, all-powerful Supreme Being, how did the writer know that another animal with one, but not both, of those characteristics wouldn't be discovered in Australia or North America? Especially since neither of those places had been "discovered" when the Torah was written.

Do You Have Any Other Suggestions For Connecting To G-d?

Study the Torah. If you study the Torah with a rabbi who can bring out its beauty, you can't help but believe in *Hashem*. The Torah is not a history book that tells a story from creation to the death of Moses. It is a book of instructions on how to conduct our lives. Every single sentence can be interpreted on different levels, with each interpretation giving us insight on how to get the most out of life. Pick up the Stone Edition of the *Chumash*, the first five books of the Torah, and read a few paragraphs. Then read the footnotes. If you're not shaking your head saying, "I never knew that!" over and over again, I'll refund the purchase price of the book. Okay, so I got carried away. It's just that every Jew can experience a unique quantity and quality of excitement that can only be found by studying the Torah.

I'm Not Sure I Believe In G-d.

Every Jew believes in *Hashem* on some level. Rambam, one of our great sages, equates our knowledge that *Hashem* exists with our knowledge of the fact that we couldn't exist for more than a few moments without oxygen. Ask a child where rain comes from and he will inevitably tell you "from G-d." No one tells him that, he just knows. Growing up tends to subvert our natural instincts.

It's Funny, But I Remember Believing In G-d When I Was A Kid.

We all did. There is a story about a rabbi who asked a child, "Where can *Hashem* be found?" The child replied, "Everywhere. Up, down and all around." The rabbi countered: "He can only be found where you allow Him to be found." We can find *Hashem* in every aspect of our lives. Unfortunately, as we grow older, we tend to find Him in fewer and fewer places.

How Do You Get Back That Child-like Assurance That G-d Exists?

Don't give up. The more you expose yourself to authentic *Yiddishkeit* (Judaism), the more you'll develop an inner awareness that Hashem exists. It may not come at first, but if you stick with the program you will ultimately come to that realization. I remember when I first started going to *shul*, and I heard the prayers being sung to melodies that I had obviously never heard before. From somewhere deep inside, I was able to hum along. Not perfectly, but close enough to make me realize that I was *not* hearing them for the first time. Just as fish instinctively know how to swim, Jews instinctively know how to relate to their Creator.

Are You Sure You Want to Define G-d As The "Creator"?

It's not a bad place to start. Either everything that has ever existed in the universe is the result of random events, or a Supreme Being has ultimate control over everything that has happened, is happening and will happen. It can't be a combination of both theories. If you come to the conclusion that *Hashem* exists, then it follows that He created us.

Maybe A Supreme Being Got Things Started, And Then Split?

Think of it this way. Would a responsible parent abandon a child he loves? Of course not. *Hashem* only wants what's best for us. To insure that happens, He stays involved with us on a moment-by-moment basis.

Then Why Don't All Jews Accept G-d Into Their Lives?

Why don't small children always obey their parents? They just don't. But as children get older, they realize they have certain responsibilities to obey their parents while they are living in their parents' home. Similarly, we have a responsibility to investigate and then obey the guidelines *Hashem* has established for us (i.e. the Torah) as long as we are living in His world.

So People Don't Believe In G-d Because They're Stubborn?

That could be a part of the reason. On some level, we all understand that we are required to submit to rules established by others. We follow the directives of our employers and the "rules of the road" without a second thought. Some people who deny the existence of *Hashem* may simply be afraid of taking on the responsibilities incumbent upon someone who is dependent upon another.

Some Of Us Just Don't Think About The Concept Of G-d At All.

That's probably more common than outright denial. On a day-to-day basis, most people don't think about macro concepts like the existence of a Supreme Being or the purpose of life. These concepts are usually examined only when a tragic event occurs, or when someone gets to a point in life where they have achieved most of their material goals. In either case, they may start wondering what they are living for. If someone never truly experiences tragedy or emptiness, chances are they won't seriously examine their lives in any real detail.

Everyone Goes Through Tough Times.

But it doesn't always motivate us to change the way we live. One aspect of being Torah observant is that we are asked to constantly examine events that take place in our lives. Although we can't determine the precise reason *Hashem* causes an event to take place, the process of looking for significance makes us extremely aware of the world around us, and how we behave toward others. One of the great benefits of being Jewish is that we have rabbis who can use the Torah to explain to us the cause, and proper response, to important events that take place in our lives.

Why Do We Need Rabbis To Help Us Interpret The Torah? Why Can't We Figure It Out On Our Own?

Rabbi Amnon Yitzchak has an explanation. He is a famous rabbi in Israel who works with Jews like us, and he is often asked the same question. Rabbi Yitzchak gives a lot of speeches, and when he wants to leave, he winks to his driver to get ready to go. You and I would only see the rabbi blinking his eye, and would perhaps think that he has some dust in it. But his driver, who has been working with Rabbi Yitzchak for many years, knows that in exactly ten minutes they are going to be leaving. In the same way, our rabbis have spent decades studying the Torah. *Hashem* is constantly winking at us, but since most of what we are learning is new to us, we need our rabbis to interpret what *Hashem* is saying.

Enough Already. I'm Convinced. Just Tell Me What Hashem *Wants From Me?*

It's kind of like the Army slogan, "Be all that you can be." We all have specific challenges to work through. What *Hashem* wants from me is totally different from what He wants from my *rebbe* or from you or from anyone else. What we all have in common is the need to study the Torah and live to the best of our abilities according to the commandments He has provided for us.

That's Easy For You To Say.

Stay with me. This is the best part. The absolutely most rewarding aspect of accepting the fact that *Hashem* runs the world is knowing that He loves me and only wants what's best for me. Before I started learning, I experienced a number of setbacks. Had these disasters not occurred, I might have been swallowed up by popular culture. More recently, there was a business opportunity that I thought would be quite lucrative. The downside was that I would have to be away from home at least three days each week. In the six months since that opportunity did not materialize, I had the time to pray and learn on a regular basis, and other business opportunities became available. Plus, I had the time to write this book.

I want to emphasize this point. If we can interpret every event that touches us as being for our benefit, we can reach an amazing state of inner peace. It is an incredible way to go through the day. Even if our first reaction is to get upset, as quickly as possible we should remind ourselves that *Hashem* runs the world, that He has our best interests in mind in all that He does for us, and that He is most probably sending us a message.

Sorry, I Didn't Hear That Last Point, My Boss Is Screaming At Me.

This is a test, and only a test. *Hashem* does a lot of that. He puts us in situations where we can either act according to the teachings of the Torah (patiently, find out what is bothering your boss and deal with it rationally), or act emotionally without thinking of the consequences (scream back). *Hashem* does not give us challenges that we can't handle. The key for me has been to acknowledge the challenge and say, "I can deal with this." It doesn't always work right away, but every challenge intensifies my consciousness of *Hashem's* presence in my life. In addition, many challenges have helped me realize that I have abilities I wasn't aware of, since I know I have the ability to successfully meet every challenge.

We Covered A Lot Of Material. Could You Please Summarize the Main Points?

I 'd be glad to.

1. Every Jew "knows" that *Hashem* exists.

2. Because *Hashem* created us, we have certain responsibilities to Him.

3. If you don't already believe in *Hashem*, take a hard look at the world around you.

4. If you still don't believe, go to a Discovery Program.

5. If you still don't believe, talk to a rabbi.

6. If you still don't believe, check your pulse.

7. Everything that happens to us is for our benefit.

8. Challenges are designed to be overcome.

9. Overcoming challenges makes us stronger.

10. Accepting challenges as being from *Hashem* and for our benefit will increase your peace of mind.

From FEAR to ETERNITY

Step Four

Pick Up Your Diamonds

Step 4: Pick Up Your Diamonds

Imagine a remote tropical island inhabited by a tribe that had no contact with the outside world. They were ignorant but happy. Only one thing disturbed their idyllic lifestyle: wherever they walked, little stones with sharp edges became embedded into their bare feet.

One day, a ship landed on the island. The passengers could not believe what they saw. The little stones were diamonds. In a short time, all of the diamonds that had been lying on the ground were picked up. The passengers then started sifting through sand, and found still more diamonds. Eventually, they were digging through volcanic rock to find the biggest and most valuable diamonds.

We are walking around in a world covered in diamonds. Some of those diamonds are right under our noses; some can be obtained with a little work; and, as with anything else, the most valuable ones are the most difficult to obtain.

What Are You Talking About?

Mitzvahs (Torah commandments).

Mitzvahs *Are As Valuable As Diamonds?*

No. They are more valuable. Diamonds have no intrinsic value. If we all woke up tomorrow and decided that engagement rings should have granite in the setting, diamonds would be nothing more than hard rocks. They have a material value in this world that is based on what the market decides they are worth. They do not inherently make our lives better. The proof? Many people with a substantial net worth are not inherently happy—few are, most aren't.

Contrast this with those Jews who observe *mitzvahs.* They are inherently living a life of fulfillment. Doing *mitzvahs* will, by definition, make your life more fulfilling. Plus, they go into the "*mitzvah* bank" in the World To Come.

The World To Come?

It's beyond the scope of this book. I remember growing up thinking that Jews believed that when you die, you die. The truth is vastly different. In very simple terms, we believe that when we die, all of our thoughts, words and actions are judged. That our souls have the potential to remain for eternity in an exalted state (the World to Come), the benefits of which are beyond our wildest imaginations. The ultimate purpose of life is to gain admittance to the World to Come.

What's The Game Plan For Getting Into The World To Come?

Getting in touch with the real you. We believe that all Jews have an understanding of the Torah embedded in their subconscious. The fact that we are thinking about what being Jewish is really all about, in spite of growing up without any real appreciation of the benefits, is proof that we all have a "*pintella yid*"—a Jewish spark—deep inside of us. Our goal is to get our conscious state (the way we act) in tune with our subconscious state (the way we're supposed to act).

What If There Is No World To Come? Why Should I Change My Life?

Good question. If there is a World to Come and the To-rah is the road map on how to get there, then one would certainly have no regrets about living according to the To-rah. But what if all of the Jewish Sages for the last 3,000 years have been wrong?

We're still better off living according to the laws set down in the Torah. Why? Because it guarantees that we'll have a more fulfilling life. Sure, we'll have to give up bacon cheeseburgers, but we'll have a better shot at a great marriage and having lots of productive children. We'll have more holidays to celebrate and at least one full day off every week that we can spend with our family and close friends. We'll be part of an incredibly supportive community.

Put another way, if we live as a Torah observant Jew and there is no World to Come, what have we given up? On the other hand, if we don't live according to the Torah and there is a World to Come, we have just wasted a lifetime of opportunities for insuring that we will be welcomed into eternity with open arms.

Come On, It's Not That Simple. I'd Have To Change My Entire Life!

Let's talk about what makes life worth living. A basic tenet of an observant lifestyle is that our satisfaction, our sense of self worth comes from doing for others, raising children we can be proud of, and otherwise trying in our own small way to make a positive impact on the world in which we live. No one said it's easy. In addition to the challenges every one of us faces, such as making a living, observant Jews are asked to *daven* (pray) and learn Torah; to avoid eating at certain restaurants; to invite guests into our home; and to engage in many other activities that leave us absolutely exhausted at the end of the day. What makes it even more challenging is that we are asked to take on all of these challenges with a smile, because we are doing what Hashem wants, not just what we want. But the payoff is more than worth the effort—or as my friends in the military say, "The juice is worth the squeeze."

You Mean My Life Is Going To Get More Difficult?

Goals related to finding self-worth are not easy to accomplish. But because we have an objective set of guidelines (that is, the Torah) on how to best accomplish them, it can be done. In addition, finding self-worth by helping others is much more satisfying than maximizing one's own financial position, concentrating on the pursuit of luxuries, and so on.

What If We Don't Get Into The World To Come?

Most likely we'll be coming back to this world. Facing all of the challenges we were unable to overcome in this life.

What's So Bad About That?

See if this story helps. Imagine that a man left his wife and kids to go work on the Alaska pipeline for five years. After amassing a substantial sum of money, he boards a boat to come home. He sees a sign as he is getting on the boat that says: *You must pay all debts incurred in Alaska or you will not be allowed to disembark.* The man thinks to himself, "Okay, so I owe my barber a couple of bucks and a real estate agent a small fee. It's no big deal."

After a long journey, the boat finally docks in his hometown. He sees his wife and kids for the first time in five years. They are waving and shouting and crying tears of joy. As he's about to disembark, an official tells him he has to return to Alaska to pay his debts.

The man screams, "I'm rich, just take the money! Take ten times the money I owe, just let me be with my family!"

"Sorry, you have to go back," says the official.

That is how we will feel if we have to come back to this world after a glimpse of the World to Come.

What Were You Saying About The Mitzvah *Bank?*

Hashem **rewards us for doing** *mitzvahs.* Think of it this way. Employees are primarily compensated with a paycheck which is deposited in a financial institution. Employees are also entitled to fringe benefits like health insurance, an IRA and paid vacation. When we do a *mitzvah,* the primary reward or "paycheck" goes into the "*mitzvah* bank" which *Hashem* keeps for us in the World to Come. We live off the interest on our deposits into the *mitzvah* bank. In other words, the fringe benefit of performing *mitzvahs* is that they enhance our everyday lives. For instance, statistics show that traffic fatalities occur more proportionately during *Shabbos* than any other day of the week. Accordingly, one of the fringe benefits of not driving on *Shabbos* is not subjecting ourselves to that risk.

64

You Can't Use What's In The Mitzvah Bank To Pay The Rent.

At least not in this world. When you get to the World to Come, your balance in the "*mitzvah* bank" will determine how you will be spending eternity. The question you have to ask yourself is, are you accumulating enough *mitzvahs* to spend eternity with a penthouse view of the ocean at sunset? Or will you be a homeless vagrant?

Prior to World War II, the acknowledged leader of Torah observant Jews throughout the world was the Chofetz Chaim, Rabbi Yisroel Meir Kagan of Radin, Poland. Notwithstanding his brilliance and acclaim, he chose to live simply. Very simply.

A rich man who came to visit him asked, "Rabbi, where is your furniture?"

The Chofetz Chaim replied, "Where is yours?"

"I am only visiting," the man said. "It would be a waste of my time and valuable resources to take my furniture with me on such a short excursion."

The Chofetz Chaim countered, " I too am only here for a short visit. In the World to Come, my *mitzvahs* are building a mansion with exquisite furniture in every room."

Don't Worry, I've Done Plenty Of Good Deeds.

That's not exactly how we translate the word *mitzvah*. The word *mitzvah* actually means "commandment." For example, we are commanded to observe *Shabbos*. It's not just a good deed that we are rewarded for doing. It is a commandment that we bear responsibility for not performing.

But I'm A Nice Person.

That's nice ... but not necessarily relevant. Often when we do something "nice" for someone, we have an ulterior motive. We are doing it so the other person will like us, or honor us, or repay us sometime in the future. Therefore, when we do something "nice" for someone else, it is not necessarily a *mitzvah*—unless its roots can be traced to the Torah.

Are All Mitvahs Referenced In The Torah?

Yes. *Mitzvahs* can be categorized into directives to perform a particular action (a "positive *mitzvah*") or directives to refrain from performing a particular action (a "negative *mitzvah*"). By performing positive *mitzvahs* in the manner that they are prescribed and by not transgressing the negative *mitzvahs*, we can get the most out of every facet of our lives.

What Do You Mean By "Every Facet Of Our Lives?"

Literally and figuratively, every way you can think of. *Mitzvahs* are designed for our benefit, even though they may not appear that way until we have actually taken them on. For instance, even after I had been going to Torah classes for over two years, I couldn't imagine keeping the laws of *Shabbos*. I couldn't comprehend the benefits, and I couldn't imagine living without what I would be giving up. And then I experienced a true *Shabbos* at the home of my *rebbe* and discovered why so many people make such a big deal out of keeping *Shabbos*. I eat three great meals with highly intelligent people. I hear at least one class from an inspired and inspiring rabbi. I take long walks and even longer naps. I visit with friends. What am I giving up? Drinking in a smoky bar on Friday night, playing racquetball on Saturday afternoon and watching television.

The bottom line: every single *mitzvah* in the Torah is designed to make our lives more pleasurable.

Mitzvahs *Will Make My Life More Pleasurable?*

Without a doubt. But first you have to become a connoisseur. Someone who appreciates a good bottle of wine will be able to tell you how the grapes were grown, what the weather was like in the year they were harvested, the bottling process, the type of earth the grapes were grown in and what additives were used. They will examine the wine's bouquet, swirl around the glass and look at the trails the wine leaves on the inside of the glass. Finally, they will taste it—though not by drinking it down in one gulp. They will savor every drop.

You can't start performing *mitzvahs* and immediately expect to get as much out of them as someone who has studied their significance, performs them on a regular basis and is motivated to action by a sincere interest in doing what *Hashem* has commanded us to do.

Run That By Me Again.

I'd be glad to. We get more out of most *mitzvahs* when they become more comfortable for us. That only occurs over time, and through repetition. The goal is to experience unadulterated joy when performing each *mitzvah*. Can I get excited about going to sleep at night—not because I'm tired, but because *Hashem* wants me to get enough sleep, so I can get up the next morning with the energy to pray the morning blessings properly? Can I take advantage of each opportunity to treat my parents with greater respect? Our Sages teach us that we can actually sense a feeling of connection to a higher place when we do *mitzvahs* properly. It is referred to as the "enveloping light."

I Can't Afford To Devote So Much Of My Time To Being Jewish.

I can't afford not to. Someone recently said that I spend too much time on my Jewishness, as if I should spend 30% of my time working, 25% sleeping, 20% with family, 10% on recreation and 15% on being Jewish. When we adopt a *mitzvah* observant lifestyle, 100% of our lives are affected in a positive way by our Jewishness.

Think of it this way. Life can be very challenging. Fortunately, we come with an owner's manual. Why not make things easier for ourselves and use it?

An Owner's Manual?

How about some analogies. Could you program a VCR or navigate the intricacies of a new software program without directions? If your car stops running, the first thing you do is review the owner's manual.

We come equipped with an incredibly detailed set of instructions for living life to its fullest. Not only is it the blueprint for our very existence, but also for the existence of every person, place, situation and object with which we will ever come in contact.

It Must Be New, Because I've Never Heard Of It.

Actually, it has been around for over 3,000 years.
The word Torah means "instructions." The Torah gives us a road map on how to handle every imaginable situation, from the moment we wake up in the morning until we put our heads on our pillows each night. It guides us through relationships with parents, teachers, spouses, siblings, friends and business associates. It has something to teach us about every event that occurs in our lives. Especially the events that seem like coincidences.

I Suppose You're Going To Tell Me There Are No Coincidences

Exactly. Everything that happens to us is designed for our benefit, to move us closer to *Hashem.*

I'd Love To Be Closer To Hashem.

Start doing *mitzvahs.* Although doing *mitzvahs* will enhance our lives in this world and improve our position in the World to Come, the primary reason we do *mitzvahs* is to get closer to *Hashem.*

So, Which Mitzvahs Should I Do First?

It's your choice, but I'd recommend ...

The easy ones. We all have certain *mitzvahs* that are easy for us, based on the type of people we are. This is not to say that we should wait decades to take on *mitzvahs* that are more difficult for us. It's just that taking on *mitzvahs* is a process, and it's best to take on the easy *mitzvahs* first. There is an obvious benefit to this approach. The sense of accomplishment that we feel from taking on easy *mitzvahs* gives us the confidence to eventually take on the more difficult ones.

The ones you can commit to. Take on each *mitzvah* with the idea that it is a permanent commitment. It is much easier to stick with something if you're not just trying it out.

The important ones. There are certain *mitzvahs* which publicly declare that "we're open for business" as Jews. These *mitzvahs* openly proclaim that we are Jews who believe in *Hashem* and the Torah.

Can You Be More Specific? Where Should I Start?

Kashrut. Everyone will tackle this *mitzvah* a little differently. Here are my suggestions.

Step 1. The starting place should be to give up pork and shellfish. Since most people aren't eating lobster every day, this shouldn't be that big of a sacrifice.

Step 2. Most people would be amazed to find out how easy it is to keep their homes stocked with kosher food. First of all, many of the brands you are already eating are kosher. Everything from Coke to Lays Potato Chips to Cheerios to Orville Redenbacher popcorn is kosher. For the brands you are used to buying that aren't kosher, there is almost always a kosher equivalent, including kosher bacon bits. The key is to be able to recognize the *hechsherim*—the symbols that designate kosher certification that appear on the labels of many foods.

Step 3. Buying kosher meat for your home is also going to be easier than you think. Grocery stores in most major cities stock kosher brands of chicken, turkey and cold cuts, so the major hassle will be finding a kosher butcher that sells red meat.

Step 4. To make your home kosher, you will need the assistance of an observant rabbi. You will need to get rid of some plastic and pottery and immerse certain glass and metal items in the *mikvah* (ritual bath). It will also entail using separate utensils, pots, pans and plates for milk and meat, which may be a bit confusing at first. You'll get used to it fairly quickly.

Step 5. Eating out is a big challenge. The usual progression is to first give up eating pork and shellfish (leaving everything else). Then you can cut out non-kosher meat (leaving fish, pasta and salads). Then you can give up food that has to be cooked (leaving salads). At some point you can restrict eating in non-kosher restaurants to business meetings. Again, ask a rabbi for the best approach for you.

Is That How You Proceeded?

Not exactly. First, I gave up lobster, crab and other shellfish. Since I am allergic and ended up in the hospital every time I so much as touched shellfish, it wasn't much of a sacrifice. Then I gave up eating pork products. After complying with these two basic prohibitions, I gave up eating milk and meat together. I found it was not very difficult to have a hamburger instead of a cheeseburger, or to have eggplant lasagna instead of meat lasagna. After that, I gave up non-kosher meat, which meant going to a kosher butcher for the meat I occasionally cooked at home. At that point, I was only eating fish or vegetarian pasta in restaurants. I started buying only kosher food for my house, but would occasionally have a pizza delivered. I rationalized this by using paper plates and plastic knives and forks with anything that wasn't kosher that I brought into the house. Then I had a rabbi make my kitchen kosher, and I cut out the pizza deliveries. Becoming kosher didn't happen overnight—at least for me.

What Other Mitzvahs Should I Undertake That Show I'm "Open For Business"?

Shabbos. I could use the rest of this book and still couldn't come close to accurately describing all of the benefits of observing *Shabbos.* Observing *Shabbos* has had the most profoundly positive impact on my life of any of the *mitzvahs* that I have undertaken.

To Me Shabbos Is All About What You Can't Do.

That's the best part. *Shabbos* is a day of rest, but not the conventional definition of rest that we are familiar with. The Torah defines 39 different categories of *work* that are prohibited on *Shabbos.* In addition, our rabbis have established certain *fences* around these categories that make it easier for us to avoid engaging in a prohibited activity. For instance, we are not allowed to write on *Shabbos.* To make sure we don't start doodling by mistake, we are not allowed to touch a pen or a pencil. As to why we can't drive, we are prohibited from making a fire. The spark generated by starting an engine constitutes "making a fire."

Hey, I Love To Take A Nap On Saturdays.

That's a great way to miss the point. I usually take a nap every *Shabbos* afternoon, so I don't want to sound hypocritical, but someone who avoids "working" on *Shabbos* by sleeping the day away has missed the point of *Shabbos.* By the Torah's definition, "resting" means I am divesting myself of the demands involved in making a living. I am not fighting to acquire material goods. By "resting" on *Shabbos*, I am able to spend quality time with *Hashem*. I am able to focus on what is truly important to me. I am able to communicate with my family and friends on subjects that assist me in examining the quality and direction of my life.

I have friends who are not observant who say they "rest" on *Shabbos* by not going to the office. But if I press them a bit, they admit it is not really a restful day for them. They are still running around doing errands, working on home-improvement projects and fighting for parking spaces at the mall. You cannot experience the benefits of *Shabbos* until you divest yourself of the demands of acquiring material goods.

You Got Me. I Do Drive On Shabbos.

Remember our first rule for taking on *mitzvahs*. Take on the easy *mitzvahs* first. We don't turn on lights on *Shabbos*, so unscrew the overhead light bulb in your car to keep it from going on and off every time you open the car door. We don't start an electrical current, so don't turn on the radio. We don't transact (buy and sell) so don't go shopping. As time goes on, you'll feel the need to drive less and less.

What About Driving To the Synagogue On Shabbos?

Let me start with a story. King A bet King B $1 million that he could get King B's prime minister to take off his clothes in public. To set up the bet, King B sent his prime minister to deliver a message to King A—without telling him what was really behind it. Before his prime minister left, King B told him, "Whatever you do, don't take off your clothes in public." King A accused King B's prime minister of being a hunchback. The prime minister vehemently denied the accusation. King A said, "I'll bet you $500,000 that you're a hunchback." The prime minister knew a good deal when he saw one, and decided to disrobe to prove he wasn't a hunchback. The prime minister thought King A would love the $500,000 he had earned for the kingdom. He didn't know that his actions had actually cost his King $1 million.

Hashem has decreed that we shouldn't drive on *Shabbos*, but we think that praying with a congregation is more important than not transgressing that prohibition. We think we know more than the King. We don't.

So What Should I Do?

Spend *Shabbos* in an observant neighborhood. It's extremely easy to find a family who will have you at their home for *Shabbos*. Then you'll have the best of both worlds. You will avoid having to drive, and you'll get the benefit of seeing how an observant family celebrates *Shabbos* firsthand. Any observant rabbi should be able to make the arrangements for you. Besides, you can drive to the synagogue to pray three times a day on the other six days of the week without doing anything wrong.

What Are Some Of The Most Important Mitzvahs That We Do On Shabbos?

Remember that it is a day of rest. That is the main theme. As far as the positive *mitzvahs* go, the following are the most obvious:

Say *Kiddush* Over Wine. The Fourth Commandment requires us to "sanctify the Sabbath." We do that by saying *kiddush* over a cup of wine.

Light Candles. It is a *mitzvah* for every Jew to light candles. For married couples, it is incumbent upon the wife to light. If you are single, you must light whether you are male or female. Most importantly, you must light 18 minutes before sundown. Most cities publish calendars that indicate the correct time to light each week.

Eat Challah. This actually involves three separate *mitzvahs.* First, we wash our hands and say the appropriate *brachah* (blessing) known as *al natilas yadayim.* Second, immediately before eating, we say the *hamotzi* (blessing before eating bread). Third, after the meal is over, we recite *bircas hamizon* (also known as *benching*—grace after meals).

Enjoy Three Festive Meals. As at any joyous event, we serve special foods, set a beautiful table and wear nice clothes. Additionally, everyone joins in the singing of *Shabbos* songs. Jewish bookstores sell a variety of tapes and CD's that you can listen to so when *Shabbos* arrives, you'll be ready to participate.

Focus on *Shabbos.* This means keeping conversation focused on spiritual issues, not the winning streak of our favorite team. It means having appropriate topics of discussion prepared. The weekly Torah portion is a good start. It also means not watching television or answering the phone.

How Do You Remember All The Things You Can And Can't Do On Shabbos?

It doesn't happen overnight. I spent a number of *Shabbosos* (plural of *Shabbos*) in my *rebbe's* house and that definitely helped. But even after a couple of months, I was still learning some rather basic do's and don'ts. When I moved to my own apartment within walking distance from where we prayed, I was presented with many new challenges.

Ultimately I made a list of things to do and not to do which

I tried to check each Friday morning, and then once again just before I walked out the door prior to *Shabbos*.

Shabbos *and* Kashrut. *I Guess That Just About Does It.*

We're just getting started. Actually, if you were able to take on those two *mitzvahs*, plus the *mitzvahs* we're about to talk about, you would be well on your way.

Can We Discuss Some Important *Mitzvahs That Are Easy To Take On?*

You be the judge.

The Positive *Mitzvahs* Include:

Tefillin. Jewish men over the age of 13 are commanded to put on *tefillin* every morning, other than on *Shabbos* and certain holidays. *Tefillin* consist of two black leather boxes containing verses from the Torah that describe the unique bond of love between Hashem and the Jewish people. They are bound to the head and arm of adult males during morning prayers. No one could have been more uncomfortable when they first started wearing *tefillin* than I was. But over time, with the help of my *rebbe* and the members of the *Telshe Yeshiva Kollel,* I figured out the proper procedures.

Learning Torah. Learning Torah is the only learning we do for its own sake. Try to learn every day, even if it's for only 15 minutes, whether or not you're in the mood. See Step 1, *Get Into The Zone,* for a more in-depth discussion.

Tzitzis. Tzitzis look a lot like T-shirts except that they have four strings tied in an intricate series of knots that are attached to each corner. Twice a day when we read the *Shema,* we confirm the requirement to wear *tzitzis.* What most people don't realize is how easy this *mitzvah* is. *Tzitzis* come in round neck and v-neck. They come in wool and cotton. The *tzitzis* which I wear are not much different than the white undershirts I've worn my entire life. Plus, if you tuck them into your pants, no one knows you are wearing them unless you go to a locker room and have to change into your workout clothes. The first time that happened, I was a little bit nervous. After a short time, however, I was disappointed if someone didn't see my *tzitzis*.

Praying. Even a few minutes a day would be a huge *mitzvah*. See Step 5.

Mezuzahs. Twice a day in the *Shema* we recite the requirement to put *mezuzahs*, the parchment scroll inscribed with the *Shema* (not the ornamental cover), on our doorposts. This requirement is not limited to the doors leading into our homes. It includes almost every door within our homes, other than those leading into bathrooms or closets. We are required to say a blessing before affixing them. We are further required to check them at least twice every seven years to see if they are still kosher. Many Jews have gotten into the habit of touching the *mezuzah* as they walk in and out of a room. Doing so reminds us that we are always in the company of *Hashem*. Because there are some rather difficult definitions of what constitutes a "doorpost," it is advisable to ask an observant rabbi where *mezuzahs* are required in your home.

Maybe It's My Imagination, But Being Jewish Sure Sounds Expensive

Be prepared to make a small but meaningful investment. It is especially important to get *tefillin*, *mezuzahs* and other religious objects from a reliable source. There is no such thing as just going through the motions in observing *Hashem's* commandments. If what is written in your *mezuzah* is not strictly kosher, you may as well nail a rabbit's foot to your door. The best place to apply the adage of buying "only the best" is in the observance of *mitzvahs*.

I Get The Message. Well, I Guess That About Does It. You're forgetting the Negative Mitzvahs.

Shaving. We are prohibited from putting a razor against our faces. All you have to do to comply with this commandment from *Hashem* is switch to an electric razor. Shaving with an electric razor prevents you from committing a sin for each hair you cut. Not all electric razors are kosher, so you should ask an observant rabbi before making a purchase. Another commonly misunderstood *mitzvah*, related to not putting a razor to our faces, is the *mitzvah* of having *payos* (sideburns). Again, this *mitzvah* is incredible easy to comply with. All you have to do is ask your barber to cut your hair so your sideburns come to just above your earlobe. Ask an Torah observant rabbi about the precise location.

Shaatnez. We are prohibited from wearing clothes that mix wool and linen (*shaatnez*). I can tell you from personal experience that it is impossible to tell if a garment is *shaatnez* free just by reading the label. Many manufacturers use a felt backing in the collar of men's jackets that is 100% *shaatnez*. Fortunately, in most cities you can pay a nominal fee to check your clothes for *shaatnez*. In my case, quite a few of my suits had *shaatnez* in the backing of the collar that had to be replaced, also for a nominal fee. If you don't adhere to this prohibition, you could literally be committing an *aveirah* (sin) every minute you are wearing clothes.

I Don't Understand The Rationale Behind Most Of These Mitzvahs.

When you meet *Hashem*, you can ask Him. There are three types of *mitzvahs*. There are *mitzvahs* that make sense from a "judicial" standpoint, such as the prohibition against murder or the requirement that you pay damages to someone you injure. There are certain *mitzvahs*, such as *Shabbos*, that are "testimonials" to our recognition of *Hashem* and His love for us. Although we wouldn't have thought up these *mitzvahs* on our own, we can intellectually comprehend them. Then there are "statutory" *mitzvahs*, commandments that we can't understand, such as not shaving with a razor or not wearing *shaatnez*.

If we only did *mitzvahs* that made sense to us, we wouldn't be fulfilling Hashem's will—we'd be fulfilling our own will. It is extremely important to do the statutory *mitzvahs* because it shows that we are subverting our will to the will of *Hashem.* If someone happens to ask you why you are performing these *mitzvahs*, just say, "Because *Hashem* said so."

At Least I Understand Why We Keep Kosher.

I doubt it. Most of us were raised with the mistaken belief that we keep kosher for health reasons. As a result, the logic goes, because of modern packaging techniques, there is no good reason to observe this *mitzvah*. I have also heard that because slaughtering animals in accordance with Jewish law is more humane, one should buy kosher meat. This may be true, but it's not the reason we observe the laws of *kashrut.*

I had a roommate in law school that said that the real reason we keep kosher is to prevent intermarriage. His rationale was that if Jews could only eat at the homes of other Jews or at a kosher restaurant, we would not be dating non-Jews, much less marrying them. This is also a bonus, but not the reason for all the rules related to keeping kosher.

So Why Do We Keep Kosher?

Because *Hashem* said so. Eating non-kosher food causes spiritual cholesterol. It hardens the arteries that give us the ability to freely accept *Hashem* and do *mitzvahs*. Have you ever seen a Jew eat a lobster and then say Grace after Meals? Have you ever seen a Jew leave a pig roast early to go pray? Most people think food only sustains the body. The Torah teaches us that food also sustains the soul. A jet won't fly the way it was designed to if you fill it up with gasoline meant for a 1947 Chevy. Ultimately, it might crash. Think of yourself as a high performance jet that was designed by *Hashem*. Certain foods make your engine purr, and certain foods make it stall.

But Eating Non-Kosher Food Doesn't Make Us Sick

I know the argument. People argue that they eat non-kosher food and don't immediately fall over with a heart attack, as if that proves it's not bad for them. But there is a cumulative effect when you do anything that isn't in your best interests. Aside from that, *Hashem* has a delayed system of consequences for our actions. Again, the subject of those consequences is beyond the scope of this book. Suffice it to say that we don't get away with anything.

Are There Any Mitzvahs For Beginners?

How about saying "please" and "thank you." There is

an elaborate system of thanking *Hashem* for the pleasures we receive. There are blessings that we say both before and after eating every meal. We say a blessing when we get up in the morning as thanks for giving us another day. We say a blessing when we go on a trip to ask that we may arrive safely and accomplish our goals. We say a blessing when we put on a new suit of clothes or hear unusually good news.

Does Hashem *Really Need Us To Bless Him?*

We aren't. By beginning each blessing with "Blessed are you, *Hashem*, our G-d, King of the Universe," we are acknowledging the fact that *Hashem* is the source of all blessings. That everything flows from Him. In fact, the word for "Jew" in Hebrew is "*Yehudi*" which comes from "*Yehudah*," which means "thankful." Being thankful, especially acknowledging all of the benefits that *Hashem* bestows upon us, is one of the most obvious characteristics of any Jew.

Having To Say *"Please"* and *"Thank You"* All The Time Sounds Oppressive.

Your mom wouldn't agree. She made you say "thank you" because she didn't want you to take what she, and others, gave you for granted—not because she needed to hear you say it. Saying "thank you" makes you appreciate what others do for you.

Can't I Have Any Fun?

You're obligated to have fun. The Torah specifically says that you are obligated to perform *mitzvahs* with joy. I have been to a lot of parties over the years, and I have never experienced the unrestrained joy that goes on around a *Shabbos* table laden with delicacies, or at the wedding of an observant Jewish couple. Plus, the entire system of observing *mitzvahs* is guaranteed to make your life more fulfilling and your day-to-day life more enjoyable. When you are constantly accomplishing worthwhile goals, you are inherently more joyful. Such is the life of someone who makes a concerted effort to live according to the Torah. Having said that, it is a pity if someone goes to the trouble of observing *mitzvahs* without experiencing any real joy. Sort of like trying to enjoy your favorite meal without taste buds.

It All Seems So Overwhelming.

Just remember, every *mitzvah* you do counts. Even if you don't do a particular *mitzvah* all the time. Even if you don't do each *mitzvah* with the proper intentions, or if you get frustrated and quit and then start again. Even if it takes you years to take on a particular *mitzvah*. Don't get discouraged. *Every mitzvah counts.*

I Hate To Admit This, But I'm A Little Scared.

I know the feeling. What I've found is that the fear associated with taking on a *mitzvah* is much worse than the discomfort I felt once in actually performing the *mitzvah*. This is true whether it was a *mitzvah* I did in the privacy of my own home, or one I did publicly.

A good example is not going to non-kosher restaurants with my family and friends. Not only did I genuinely enjoy those events, but I had built up a lot of fears about distancing myself from people I had always been close with. When I finally made the decision, my friends responded by saying, "What took you so long? We knew it was coming sooner or later." My mother koshered enough of her kitchen so I felt comfortable eating there, and when I went to visit my sister, she was ready with a kosher meal. More than one of my friends offered to pick up a kosher pizza to entice me to their homes for a meal. I will admit that my transition was made easier by having a supportive family and understanding friends. But universally, the fear of taking on a *mitzvah* is much worse than any negative experience you will encounter once you have accepted a *mitzvah* upon yourself.

Any Final Words Of Wisdom On Mitzvahs?

From me, no. From our sages, yes. We are encouraged to find a *mitzvah* or two that we can "specialize" in. One that we can really take to heart and make an integral part of our lives. It may be something that comes easily to us because of the way we were raised, or it could be some special connection to the Jewish faith that we recently discovered. For instance, I love *Shabbos* and try to make each one special. Some people have found that the prohibition of *loshon hora*, gossip and slander, is one that they relate to, because they have always followed the rule, "If you can't say something nice about someone, don't say anything at all." Visiting the sick or helping young couples make weddings or assisting the elderly are all possibilities. You just have to find the *mitzvah*(s) that have a special meaning to you.

One More Question. What About People Who Don't Undertake Mitzvahs Who Have Great Lives?

You mean, "Why do good things happen to bad people?" First, you never know what is going on behind closed doors. To our untrained eyes, it seems that some people, especially celebrities, lead exquisite lives. However, they are often beset with personal problems that are mind-boggling. Second, some people do live relatively stress free for the majority of their lives, only to unfortunately experience tragedy after tragedy in their declining years. Third, it's possible that *Hashem* is compensating them in this world, as opposed to the World to Come, for all of the *mitzvahs* they performed. Even people who lie and cheat and steal also perform acts of kindness, such as being nice to their parents or occasionally giving charity. If they enjoy a relatively pleasurable existence in this world, they may be depleting the reward they would have otherwise received for those *mitzvahs* in the World to Come. You could put what I know about the World to Come on the head of a pin and still have room left over for what I know about *mitzvahs*. But I do know that you don't want to arrive in the World to Come with no deposits in the "*mitzvah* bank."

Step Five

Turn On The Faucet

Step 5: Turn on the Faucet

R emember the people living on the remote island who didn't know the value of diamonds? Imagine that the captain of the ship who discovered them brought a couple of the islanders back to civilization. When the ship arrived, the captain was very busy. He dropped the islanders off at his home and said he'd be back in a few days. He left some food out on the kitchen counter and assumed they would make themselves at home.

When he finally came back, the islanders were almost dead from thirst—because they hadn't had anything to drink during all the days that he had been gone. The captain stared at them in disbelief. He turned on the kitchen faucet and cool, life-sustaining water gushed forth. The islanders' lack of education had created a life-threatening situation.

Again, we are the islanders. *Hashem* has created a system whereby all of our material, physical and spiritual needs can be met. All we have to do is *turn on the faucet*.

And How Do We Do That?

By praying. Think of it this way. There is a huge reservoir filled with everything we could ever want: good health, long life, great children, wealth, and wonderful relationships with our families. Everything. Praying, in addition to reminding ourselves that there is a Supreme Being, is the primary way with which we access that reservoir. It's how we open the faucet.

And *Hashem* will consider our requests anytime we pray.

We don't have to be in *shul*. It doesn't have to be Rosh Hashanah or Yom Kippur. We don't even have to be praying with a *minyan*—a quorum of at least ten men over the age of 13 required for formal prayer in the synagogue. All we have to do is take the time to ask.

I'm Not Dying of Thirst And I Don't Pray.

Other people are praying for you. Observant Jews pray three times every day. The basic prayer, in which we ask *Hashem* for wisdom, health, forgiveness, financial security, protection and all of our other personal needs (and the needs of mankind in general), is called the *Amidah*. This silent prayer has 19 requests, but one of its central themes is a communal prayer for the entire Jewish nation and, indeed, the entire world—not just for "me." So, at least three times a day, 365 days a year, hundreds of thousands of observant Jews from all over the world are praying for you.

Sounds Like A Good System. What Should We Talk About Next?

Getting the most out of the system as it's designed. Would you let one of your co-workers go to your boss and ask for a raise for you because you were a little busy that day? Of course not. You would want to plead your own case. Although other people are praying for you, *Hashem* wants to hear from you directly.

Where Do I Start?

How about returning the favor. Our Sages teach us that we should pray for others as well as for ourselves. If you are looking for a marriage partner, pray that your friend should also find the right person. If you need assistance in making your business successful, pray for the financial success of your friends and family. One of the best ways to train ourselves to always want the best for our friends and neighbors is to pray for them.

Come To Think Of It, There's This One Sale That Could Make My Entire Year.

Try not to be so specific. Only *Hashem* really knows what's good for us, especially in the long run. Give Him some discretion in how He helps you out. For instance, it's better to pray for a general level of income to support you and your family, rather than for success in any specific endeavor, because the ramifications of success in that particular endeavor could be problematic for you in the future.

That's not to say that before going into an important meeting, you shouldn't pray for success. On the contrary! Praying is certainly worthwhile in this case. One way to approach such a situation is to ask *Hashem* to give you the intelligence to think your presentation through clearly, and that your words should be conveyed in a convincing manner. We are obligated to put in the effort; the results are up to *Hashem.*

How About If I Pray For The Intelligence To Pick The Winning Numbers For The Lottery?

We can pray for anything we want. But before deciding whether we should win the lottery, or receive any other advantage, *Hashem* first determines whether or not it will actually benefit us. A man who had been destitute his entire life came to the well-known sage, the Chofetz Chaim, and asked for a blessing that he should become wealthy. The Chofetz Chaim was reluctant. He explained to the man that *Hashem* was providing him with a level of income that was perfect for him. But the man persisted, and ultimately got his blessing. A short time later, the man came into a substantial amount of money. Within a few months, though, he had spent all of the money, mostly on frivolous items. He then felt worse than ever. He went back to the Chofetz Chaim, who explained to him that *Hashem* had determined what level of income was appropriate for him. All the man had gotten was an advance on the funds he was to receive in the future. Accordingly, what each of us should pray for is a level of income that is in our best interest, and not at the expense of any income we are destined to receive at some other time.

I'd Like To Take On The Challenge Of Sudden Wealth.

Perhaps you will. Receiving a large amount of money in a short amount of time would certainly change anyone's life. But would our relationships with friends and family be affected in a positive way? Would our kids retain the same values? Would we continue to be as dedicated to our employers? Would we be less diligent in our observance of *mitzvahs*? What new temptations might we succumb to?

Okay. But I Have A Great Deal For Hashem. *I Won't Drive On* Shabbos *If He Will ...*

Hashem doesn't make deals for things we're supposed to do. I used to try to bargain with Hashem. I would say to myself, "I'll take on a certain *mitzvah* if You help me close a certain deal." But Hashem doesn't work that way. The Torah teaches us that we are not allowed to "test"

Hashem, except when it comes to charity. If someone wanted to commit to give more charity than they are obligated to give, they could pray for something in exchange. The mechanics of this are a little tricky, so you should ask a rabbi/*rebbe* about the particulars.

I Have A Better Deal For Hashem. I Could Trade Some Of The Credit I'll Be Receiving In The World To Come From My Mitzvahs In Exchange For ...

That would be the worst deal of all time. Our Sages teach us that the smallest amount of pleasure in the World to Come is exponentially greater than the most exquisite pleasure in this world. Moreover, we are told that one of the worst punishments is having *Hashem* pay us up in this world for the *mitzvahs* that we have performed. When we pray, we ask *Hashem* not to decrease any merit we have coming to us in the World to Come for something we want in this world. We ask *Hashem*, whose nature it is to give freely and who always has our best interests at heart, to consider our prayers in spite of our transgressions, not because of any *mitzvahs* we may have performed. We just say, "*Hashem*, keep the faucet wide open."

I Have A Problem. I Don't Actually Spend That Much Time In Shul.

You can pray almost anywhere and at anytime. And don't be shy. Ask for assistance in every aspect of your life. Aside from when you're in a bathroom or in certain public places, you could be praying all day long. I like to have a conversation with *Hashem* when I'm driving. It's quiet and I know I won't be interrupted.

What About Praying With a Minyan?

It helps. Think of the concept of collective bargaining that underlies the union movement. It carries a lot more weight if all of a company's employees ask the boss for a raise than if one employee asks just for himself. To take this analogy one step further, if we went to our boss to plead our case, we'd want to take as many of the company's valuable employees with us so our requests would be taken as seriously as possible. A *minyan* is a *minyan*, but if you had a choice you would try to pick the *minyan* with the greatest number of people, and, if you could establish it, the *minyan* with the greatest number of righteous people.

What Percentage Of Your Prayers Are Answered?

100% if they are sincere. It's just that sometimes the answer is "no." Many times the answer is, "yes, but not right now." With our limited capacity, we can't begin to know what is best for us. *Hashem* responds to my prayers in the way that is best for me.

We also believe that no prayer is wasted. Sometimes prayers are stored away. Many great rabbis have said that the heartfelt prayers of our grandparents and great grandparents that were uttered decades ago are responsible for the many Jews who are now returning to an observant lifestyle.

I'm Not Observant. Why Should Hashem Grant Any Of My Requests?

It's His nature. *Hashem* is like every father, in that He wants all of His children to succeed. In addition, we benefit from the merits of a long line of righteous men and women who passed tests that are well beyond our abilities and imaginations. For instance, in the first paragraph of the prayer known as the *Amidah*, which we say three times a day, we ask *Hashem* to consider the merit of Abraham, Isaac and Jacob in granting our desires. By the way, you should have phrased your question slightly differently: you're "not observant ... *yet.*"

Why Can't I Pray The Way I Want To? Why Do I Have To Follow The Prayer Book?

Time after time, the system is the solution. If you wanted to apply for a grant, and could afford it, you would hire a professional grant writer whose previous requests had been favorably received. Similarly, our prayer books have been written by *tzaddikim* (righteous individuals), who knew the most expeditious manner in which to beseech *Hashem*. Free-form praying works, and if you can move yourself to tears, I would tell you it's preferred. But usually, we don't have that level of emotion in our *davening.* We all want to get to the same place. Why not travel a paved road instead of trying to blaze your own trail?

Can You Give Me A Few Tips On Praying? It's All Pretty New To Me.

Imagine you had a meeting with Bill Gates.

You would:

1. Prepare by reviewing your issues in advance.

2. Arrive early.

3. Dress in a manner that shows that you want to be taken seriously.

4. Don't engage in small talk with those around you.

5. When you are asked to read something, enunciate each word.

6. Don't rush away, as if your next meeting is more important.

This is, of course, a weak comparison. Comparing the ability of the richest man in the world to assist you with *Hashem*'s ability to assist you is like asking someone who possesses a thimble to give you some water, as opposed to someone who owns the Great Lakes.

Step Six

Prepare For The Holidays

Step 6: Prepare For The Holidays

Ａll parents have certain expressions that are meant to impart the building blocks of a successful life. Some of them are absolute truisms, such as, "What you get out of something is based on what you put into it." This is especially true when we consider the Jewish holidays.

Finally, A Subject I Can Relate To. Let's Start With Rosh Hashana. I Love Apples And Honey.

Great, but Chanukah is just around the corner. I have a million things to review. We can go over them together.

Chanukah Is A Kids' Holiday. Just Buy A Few Presents, A Menorah And Some Candles.

Chanukah has major significance for every Jew. In fact, we could fill an entire book with explanations on the basics of each of the holidays and how to prepare for them. I don't even know where to start.

How About Listing Each Of The Jewish Holidays?

It's best to put them into categories. First there are the five holidays that are mentioned in the Torah: Shavuos, Rosh Hashanah, Yom Kippur, Sukkos and Pesach. Then there are the two holidays that were inaugurated by the rabbis: Chanukah and Purim. There are five "minor" fast days, on which we fast from sunup to sundown, and one all-day fast on the ninth of the month of Av, which commemorates the destruction of the First and Second Temples and a variety of other tragic events in Jewish history. And of course, every *Shabbos* is a holiday. And there are a few others like Hoshana Rabbah and Simchas Torah.

WOW. That's A Lot Of Days At The Beach.

Jewish Holidays are not about killing time. Each holiday is an opportunity for growth that is unlike any other day in the year.

Then Why Did My Observant Friend Just Return To Work With A Tan?

He probably lived a long way from his shul. Over a two-day Jewish holiday he had to walk back and forth to the shul six times because he wouldn't drive.

Can We Please Go Over The Holidays Mentioned In The Torah And Purim and Chanakuh?

Let's do a quick summary, starting with ... PESACH

Shouldn't We Start With Rosh Hashanah—The Jewish New Year?

Pesach is where it all began. It is the founding holiday of the Jewish People. One minute we were slaves; moments later, we were free and on our way out of Egypt as a united people. It teaches us that even today, our lives can change in an instant.

It's noteworthy that Pesach occurs in the Spring—a time of new life and new beginnings. Pesach is when we work to clean our homes of *chometz*—leavened products. And, if we are observing the Pesach *mitzvahs* correctly, we are working to clean up our act as well.

I Thought The Focus Of The Holiday Was Freedom.

And now I'll tell you ... "the rest of the story." To stress its importance, the Torah states that Hashem "took you out of Egypt" fifty different times. Yes, *Hashem* did free us from our slavery to Pharaoh, but only so we could accept the Torah. He gave us the ability to serve a father figure who only wants what is best for us, instead of a dictator who wanted to destroy us. It's important to note that not every Jew left Egypt. Only the Jews who wanted to leave were part of the redemption. Only the Jews who, despite being slaves, used their Hebrew language, kept their Hebrew names and continued to dress like Jews.

I Have My Jewish Identity. I Always Eat Matzah on Pesach.

Eating matzah on Pesach for the right reasons is very important. First, there is the concept of matzah being a "poor man's bread," to remind us of the fact that we were slaves in Egypt. Second, the bread that we give up eating during Pesach—the puffy, inflated kind—reminds us of the negative aspects of our egos, which are likewise puffy and inflated.

Why Don't We Eat Bread On Pesach?

It goes way beyond not eating bread on Pesach. We are not even allowed to possess bread during the eight days of Pesach. Not in our homes or offices or cars. It is an absolute ban that is unique in Jewish law. We can have pork in our houses all year long, but not *chometz* during the eight days of Pesach. We can drop a spoonful of milk into a pot of chicken soup, and it doesn't ruin the soup if the amount of milk on the spoon is less than one sixtieth of the volume of the soup. But if we drop one crumb of bread into a soup designated for Pesach, the entire pot of soup has to be thrown out.

What's The Key Aspect Of Pesach To Keep In Mind?

Thanks. Over and over again we have to remind ourselves how blessed we are. That we are Jews. That we descended from the small minority of Jews who made it out of Egypt. That our ancestors made it through many other periods of persecution. That we have come together in countries that allow us to practice our religion openly. And so on, for every other blessing that Hashem has bestowed upon us.

Next comes ... SHAVUOS

Isn't Shavuos When Hashem Gave Us The Torah?

Sort of. *Hashem* addressed all the Jews who left Egypt at Mount Sinai. They heard the first two Commandments directly from *Hashem*, and then they heard Him transmit the other eight to Moses. It was the most dramatic event in the history of the world. Thunder. Lightning. The entire world shook. Had it been made into a motion picture, it would have won every Academy Award for drama, lighting, sound and special effects. Moses then went up on Mount Sinai to learn the Torah from *Hashem*. After forty days, he came down with the two tablets, which he broke when he saw the golden calf. Back up he went to pray to Hashem to forgive the people, and when he came down again it was Yom Kippur.

All 3 Million Jews Who Left Egypt Heard Hashem Speak To Them?

All of them. Judaism is the only religion based on a revelation to the masses, as opposed to the testimony of a single person—and that revelation has never been denied by any organized religion. It is one of the primary factors that makes Judaism unique. Wackos may deny the Holocaust, but no one has ever denied the fact that *Hashem* gave the Torah to the Jewish people at Mount Sinai.

So Why Is Shavuos Celebrated As The Giving Of The Torah If It Only Involved The Ten Commandments?

The Ten Commandments allude to the entire Torah. There are 620 letters in the Ten Commandments. Each letter corresponds to one of the 613 *mitzvahs* in the Torah that are binding on Jews and the seven *mitzvahs* that our Rabbis would ultimately establish.

Finally, we've reached ROSH HASHANAH

You Analogized Pesach To The Birth Of The Jewish People. I Think I Can Guess What Rosh Hashanah Is Analogous To.

There is no analogy to Rosh Hashanah in the secular world. First and foremost, Rosh Hashanah is the Day of Judgment. It is the day when Hashem decides what will happen next year—to every Jew and to every non-Jew. How much money we will make. Our health. Everything that we will go through, experience and feel.

How Does That Famous Prayer Go Again?

I think I know which one you mean. On Rosh Hashanah it will be inscribed, and on Yom Kippur it will be sealed: how many will pass from earth and how many will be created; who will live and who will die; who will die at his predestined time and who before his time; who by water and who by fire, who by sword, who by beast, who by famine, and who by stoning. Who will rest and who will be harried, who will enjoy tranquility and who will suffer, who will be impoverished and who will be enriched, who will be degraded and who will be exalted.

This Prayer Implies That Hashem *Is Only Deciding Big Issues Like Life and Death.*

He is making decisions down to the smallest detail. Let's use our livelihood as an example. He is deciding how many miles we have to commute. Some people commute an hour each way to work, while others can walk to work in five minutes. Some people have to leave their families to go on extended business trips, while others never go through that upheaval. He is deciding which families will need two incomes, and which families, with the same expenses, will get by with one. He is deciding how many setbacks we will have. Whether we will get depressed about our job and the extent of our depression. He is deciding how much we will pay in taxes, and if we are going to get audited. He is deciding if our boss will appreciate us and if our biggest customer will stay or leave.

This leads naturally into ... YOM KIPPUR

What A Downer.

On the contrary: what an opportunity. Imagine that you took a wrecking ball and flattened your neighbor's house. Do you think he would forgive you? When we sin, we are essentially taking a wrecking ball to *Hashem's* house, and yet He gives us Yom Kippur and a chance to be forgiven.

Do You Have Any Other Metaphors Related To Yom Kippur?

Sure. *Hashem* issues each of us a credit card. When we sin, He puts a charge on our card. On Yom Kippur, *Hashem* allows us to atone for our sins. Atonement involves confessing what we did, regretting what we did, and accepting upon ourselves not to repeat that behavior. Atonement is like sending a check to pay off the balance on our credit card.

What About During the Year?

Good catch. Throughout the year, we can atone for our sins, but the purification process is very difficult and time consuming, and our souls remain contaminated. On Yom Kippur, if you properly atone, you get an automatic purification of your soul.

So Why Should I Purify My Soul During The Year?

How about another metaphor. Think of our Jewish soul as a muscle. Doing a *mitzvah* is like performing exercises that strengthens our soul, and doing a sin results in our soul being disfigured. So if we do a sin that disfigures a portion of our soul, we have to find the corresponding exercise, or *mitzvah*, that will correct it. For instance, if we read material that is not in our best interest, we would have to read material that is good for us. If we use our eyes to watch things that we might be ashamed of, we should use them to watch something that would be properly inspiring. The wonderful thing about Yom Kippur is that it allows you to skip this entire process.

The great outdoors beckons on SUKKOS

Can You Believe What G-d Does To Us on Sukkos, After What He Puts Us Through on Rosh Hashana and Yom Kippur?

Isn't it great. After judging us, especially after the way we acted last year, we might think *Hashem* would turn His back on us. He shows his great love for the Jewish people by having us dwell in a *sukkah*.

How Is Eating Dinner In A Sukkah An Expression Of Love?

Lets get a few basics out of the way. First, we are commanded to "dwell" in a *sukkah*, not just eat dinner there. That is, we should eat our meals in the *sukkah*, and adult males should sleep in the *sukkah* where and when it's feasible.

What If It's Raining?

What is it's snowing? *Hashem* is not trying to make our lives miserable. If it's raining or snowing, you are required to go inside. The point is, we think our homes protect us from the elements. We think a doctor can cure us or a lawyer can win our case for us. The holiday of Sukkos reminds us that it is *Hashem* who protects us. If *Hashem* wants the walls of your home to collapse or end up in your neighbor's yard, that is exactly what will happen. Just ask the people whose homes were devastated by Hurricane Andrew.

Isn't Sukkos to Remind Us That We Lived In Huts During The 40 Years The Jews Wandered In The Desert?

Historically, yes. But every holiday has something to teach us today about our day-to-day existence. The great rabbi, the Brisker Rav, asked a former student whom he hadn't seen in quite some time, "What have you been doing?" The student said proudly, "I got married and went into a very profitable business with my father-in-law, and my wife and I had two children." Later, the Brisker Rav asked him, "What have you been doing?" The puzzled student again replied, "I got married and went into a very profitable business with my father-in-law, and my wife and I had two children." After the Brisker Rav asked the same question for the third time, the student respectfully reminded the Brisker Rav that he had already answered the question two times. The Brisker Rav replied, "I asked what *you* have been doing. You told me what *Hashem* has been doing— that He sent you a wife and children and a good livelihood." Similarly, Sukkos reminds us that everything we have is from Him.

This one should be pretty easy ... CHANUKAH

I Know What Chanukah Means: "Festival Of Lights."

Not exactly. Chanukah means, "to rededicate." From a historical perspective, it relates to the fact that after defeating the Greeks, the Jews rededicated the Second Temple. Today, we celebrate Chanukah as a reminder to rededicate ourselves to Torah and *mitzvahs*.

I'm A Little Fuzzy On The Historical Aspects Of Chanukah.

Here are the basics. The Greeks conquered Israel during the time of the Second Temple. The Greek culture emphasized the physical, as exemplified by the Olympics. Many Jews became complacent in their observance of *mitzvahs*. They still observed, but they were a bit haphazard.

Which Is Not Something That Hashem Likes.

Exactly. The Greeks outlawed three *mitzvahs* practiced by the Jewish people: giving a male child a *bris*, the observance of *Shabbos*, and the celebration of *Rosh Chodesh*, the new month. These decrees were the last straw for a high priest by the name of Mattisyahu. He and his ten sons, along with a small group of followers, decided to fight the Greeks. Ultimately, a handful of rabbis defeated tens of thousands of professional Greek soldiers.

So We Are Celebrating A Great Military Victory.

Do you also believe in the tooth fairy? Under normal circumstances, a few rabbis can't defeat thousands of soldiers—particularly at a time when the most sophisticated weapons were swords and slingshots. We are celebrating the fact that with *Hashem's* assistance, the few can defeat the many. The weak can defeat the strong.

What About The Oil Burning For Eight Days?

It's a great testament of faith. When the Jews drove the Greeks out of Jerusalem and the Temple, a priest went into the Temple to light the Menorah and found only enough oil for one day. The next day, a priest went in and discovered that the oil was still burning. And every day for six more days, a priest found the light still burning, until the ninth day, when new and purified oil was ready. The great sages of the time accepted the testimony of the priests and decided to commemorate it with a holiday.

PURIM

Can You Summarize The Historical Context In Which Purim Took Place?

Here goes. King Achashverosh, who basically ruled the entire world, asked his wife to perform at a party for his guests. When she refused, a search was undertaken for a new queen and Esther was chosen. Soon thereafter, Haman bought the right from King Achaveraus to kill all the Jews. They held a lottery (which is the literal translation of the word "Purim") to pick the date, eleven months later, on which the Jews would all be killed. Mordechai, who was Esther's uncle, told Esther to ask the King to spare the Jews. Knowing that the fate of the entire Jewish people rested on the King's answer, Esther asked that that the Jews in Shushan, the capital city, to fast and pray for three days.

I Guess It Worked.

And how. In three days, Haman went from being the key advisor to the King to being hanged along with his ten sons.

The Jews went from vanquished to victor.

And The Jews Were Saved Because They Fasted and Prayed.

That's how *Hashem* wants us to respond to challenges to our physical existence. The main focus of Purim is to teach us to deal with adversity by coming closer to *Hashem.* Purim was the ultimate challenge because it involved a threat that every Jew on the planet would be annihilated. We all have challenges. From our peers, from our jobs, and even from our families. Purim provides the paradigm for dealing with those pressures.

But The Story Of Purim Took Place Over 2,000 Years Ago.

Even so, the prayers that we say on Purim are in the present tense. We are offering thanks and praise and recognition to *Hashem* for saving us, not just in the past, but also today. And we are publicizing to the world that He is close to us when we call out to Him.

Okay, We've Covered The Basics. Can We Go Over Some Specific Ideas On How To Prepare For The Holidays?

Here are a few suggestions:

1. Go to classes to prepare for each holiday.

2. Read the Artscroll book (from Mesorah Publications) on each holiday.

3. Review the special prayer book (*machzor*) designed for each holiday.

4. Get your rabbi/*rebbe* to go over the prayers, so you will know which prayers will be said and which ones will be skipped.

5. Stand next to someone in *shul* who will go out of his or her way to help you if you get lost.

6. For fast days, stop drinking coffee with caffeine at least three days before the holiday to minimize the caffeine withdrawal headache.

From FEAR to ETERNITY

Step Seven

Recognize Challenges
As Opportunities To Grow

Step 7: Recognize Challenges As Opportunities to Grow

Suppose someone had a dream in which they were told that throughout the next day everything they would say, do, and even think would be watched, taped and analyzed at the end of the day. How do you think he'd react?

He's running late for work and can't find his car keys. He starts to yell—and suddenly remembers that someone is watching. While driving to work, a driver cuts him off. He jams on the brakes and goes for the horn. A curse starts forming in the back of his mind—but again he catches himself. When he gets to work, there is no one answering the phones because the receptionist is out sick. He runs to answer the phone and it stops ringing just as he picks it up. He starts to slam down the receiver, and again he remembers. So goes his entire day.

He Must Have Been A Wreck By The End Of The Day!

Just the opposite. Every person dreams of having leadership qualities, with the poise necessary to handle pressure in every situation. For at least one day, this person was able to make his dream come true. Notwithstanding the difficulties he had to go through, he feels great about himself because of what he accomplished.

So What's The Point Of The Story?

There are two. The first is that this is not a hypothetical story. *Hashem is* watching and recording everything that we do, say and think. If we were constantly aware of that fact, we would be generating feelings of accomplishment throughout the day as we met each challenge. The second point is that nothing happens by accident. All of our challenges are tailor-made. We only get challenges in areas where we need to improve. Some challenges, like the ones mentioned in the story, are quite easy to decipher and offer us opportunities for growth in specific areas like controlling one's temper. Other challenges shake us to the very core of our existence and offer us opportunities to change the quality and direction of our lives. The key to the pleasure we have in this world, and the type of eternity we are building for ourselves in the World to Come, is primarily a function of how we respond to challenges.

My Eternal Life Is Based On How I React When I Lose My Keys?

Strange, isn't it. We all want to believe that we would slay the dragon and rescue the damsel in distress, but do we call to promptly cancel unneeded dinner reservation? Do we respond respectfully when an elderly person has asked the same question for the third time in five minutes? When a cashier gives us back an extra $10, do we correct the mistake? Each of these situations, and in fact all challenges, are opportunities for us to grow.

Challenges Are Opportunities?

Bingo. Let's say a great business opportunity doesn't materialize. While our natural inclination is to be disappointed, we have the ability to view it as a blessing. Why? Because it may have made it more difficult to keep

Shabbos, or perhaps put us in a situation in which we would be tempted to sin.

That Approach Seems Very Difficult To Put Into Practice.

It is. We typically look at events that do not go our way as being purely negative. The Torah mandates the opposite. Although it may take a while for us to calm down after going through a particularly uncomfortable experience, we would be taking a step in the right direction if we accept all challenges as being created for our benefit. The next step, which requires a person to be on a very high spiritual level, is to accept challenges in a positive way, as they are happening. And keep in mind that the more difficult the challenge, the greater the reward.

The Word "Difficult" Doesn't Begin To Describe Some Of My Challenges.

I know. We all have families. Most people have some fear of the unknown. That fear can be magnified when someone you love gets involved in something you know little or nothing about. Such is the case with many parents who witness their children becoming more observant. Some families are opposed, while others say, "They just want whatever will make us happy"—but can't resist throwing in an "Are you crazy?" once in a while. Keep in mind that after the yelling stops, it isn't uncommon for our mothers and sisters to start lighting *Shabbos* candles and for our fathers and brothers to occasionally say *Kiddush* or show up at *shul*.

Why Are Families Resistant To A Child Becoming More Observant?

Change. I remember when my parents dropped me off for my freshman year of college. They were crying, while I couldn't have been more joyous about starting a new adventure. There is a certain amount of separation anxiety whenever a child moves to a new phase of his or her life. In the beginning, parents may also feel some sense of being rejected—as if, by our becoming more observant, we are implicitly criticizing them for not bringing us up with more religion in our lives. In fact, of course, it is just the opposite. We recognize that most of our parents weren't raised with the exposure to Judaism that we are now getting, so how could we blame them for not passing on something that they didn't possess? As I said in the Dedication, my parents raised me to be extremely proud of being Jewish, which served as the basis for the growth I am now experiencing.

I Can Only Imagine What My Parents Will Say When I Don't Show Up For A Family Dinner.

You and everyone else who becomes more observant. When I began to observe *Shabbos*, I went to *shul* on Friday night, rather than go out to dinner with my family, which is something of a tradition when we are all in town. They were hurt and it was completely understandable. Our challenge is to not let those situations break up our families. When we choose to pass on going to a family function rather than transgress a law, we have to assure our parents and other family members that our love for them has not diminished.

My Parents Were Definitely Supportive At The Beginning Of My Journey.

And why shouldn't they be? You were learning more about your Jewish heritage and doing it in a way that made them proud to say, "My son is really enjoying that class he's taking," or "She really seems to be settling down and getting serious about her future." Your parents may have been reminded somewhat of their own parents' or grandparents' commitment to being Jewish. The one phrase we all hear at one time or another is, "Fine, be more religious, but do you have to become a fanatic?"

What Will Make Me A Fanatic In My Family's Eyes?

Food. The socialization process of many Jewish families revolves around family meals, so when you start obeying the laws of *kashrut*, some "situations" will no doubt arise. Like when you show up at your parents' house and announce that you can't eat the meatloaf your mother spent two hours preparing, because you just stopped eating non-kosher meat.

I Bet It Can Get Really Tough During The Holidays.

And how. In 40 years, I only missed spending one Passover with my parents, even though I lived in other cities for sixteen of those years. One year I even hitchhiked home from college, arriving just in time to shower before the guests showed up. It was always my favorite holiday, as my mother and father gathered a variety of people to our Seder.

Nine months after becoming *Shabbos* observant, I was faced with an incredible dilemma. The first night of Pesach was on a Wednesday night.

So?

Let me explain. We observe the first two days of Pesach (and the last two days) as a holiday. The prohibitions, including not driving, are similar to the prohibitions we follow on *Shabbos*. Since the first two days (Wednesday night through Friday night) ran right into *Shabbos*, I couldn't drive for three consecutive days. My dilemma was to either have a "kosher" Pesach (including both Seders) at the home of my *Rebbe* and then observe *Shabbos*, or, since my parents did not live near an Orthodox shul, have a family-oriented Pesach Seder/dinner at my parents' home and then be unable to celebrate the remainder of Pesach and *Shabbos* in the manner in which I had been taught.

Now I Understand.

It gets worse. My mother went out of her way and bought a kosher turkey, a kosher brisket and all sorts of other kosher delicacies that would keep my gastronomic transgressions to a minimum. My sister and brother-in-law were driving in from Detroit to join 14 other family members and friends at the first Seder. On the other hand, I had cleaned and *kashered* my home for Pesach and had spent long hours learning many of the laws from the Torah and the *Gemara* applicable to Pesach. Also, I wanted to be part of a Torah observant Pesach, with the hope that I would pick up some ideas on how to someday officiate at my own Seder. I was paralyzed.

So What Did You Do?

I went "*heter* shopping"—I looked for leniencies in Jewish law. Ultimately, I asked one of the most respected rabbinical authorities in Cleveland for his advice. He convinced me that since I was already keeping *Shabbos*, it would be inconsistent for me to violate the laws governing Pesach. Unfortunately, I waited until the last minute to tell my parents I wouldn't be joining them for Pesach.

Smooth Move.

I definitely learned from the experience. A few months later, when I decided to take on certain obligations related to *kashrut*, I asked my mom to meet me in the middle of the day. We sat and talked for a couple of hours and I explained what I was trying to accomplish—both in terms of that one particular group of *mitzvahs*, and my long-term goals. My mom's response was terrific. She immediately bought broiling pans, paper plates and plastic serving pieces. We *kashered* her stove. She then bought all new pots and pans and beautiful glass plates for me to eat on. She washes everything by hand instead of putting them in the dishwasher. She and my dad have both become accustomed to checking food labels for Kosher supervision symbols so that I am at ease when I eat in their home.

So the moral of the story is: Don't give your family a fait accompli, especially at the last minute. Give them plenty of time to get used to your new life. It is just plain common sense, and is in keeping with the spirit of the *mitzvah* of *kibud av v'aim*—honoring your father and mother.

Any Other Thoughts About Dealing With One's Family?

Yes. You will have to deal with their fear that your religious observance is going to weaken your relationship with them. You have to be patient. You have to constantly reassure them that the strongest family units are in the observant community. Most importantly, you have to make a special effort to include them in your life, not exclude them.

Aren't They Worried About Their Grandchildren?

Probably. They may think it's a little extreme to not expose our children to the benefits of fast food restaurants. They may disagree with our decision to send our children to Jewish day schools instead of public schools or private secular schools. If we decide not to have a television in our homes, we may actually be putting our parents in the uncomfortable position of defending our kids' right to watch television.

Their overall concern will be that our children will not be able to function in today's society because of the limitations they perceive that we are placing on them. I do not believe that fear is justified for two reasons. The first is because 97.5% of the United States is not Jewish, so it is impossible to grow up here and not be exposed to the rest of society. Second, although observant parents have a more expansive view of what constitutes a negative influence, the net effect is merely that children from observant homes tend to be more sheltered, in certain respects, than children from non-observant homes. They don't find out about certain aspects of the real world until they are older and, hopefully, better equipped to handle them.

What Other "Little" Challenges Did You Experience?

Embarrassment comes to mind. Notwithstanding the fact that I had passed the bar exam in three states, I soon realized that every second grader in a Jewish day school knew more about Judaism than I did. I repeatedly stumbled through the few words of Hebrew that I was required to say when I was asked to be the leader for Grace after Meals. For months, I would get lost every time I prayed. I even pretended not to be hungry because I was embarrassed that I didn't know the appropriate blessings for food that I was being offered. Not knowing how to put on *tefillin*. Refusing to be called up to the Torah because I couldn't say the blessings in Hebrew. I could go on and on.

Ouch.

I got over it. It helped that so many observant Jews were so supportive. It is as if they are rooting for us. I can't tell you how many different families on how many countless *Shabbosos* and holidays invited me to their homes. Or how many people continuously inquired about my well-being or offered me words of encouragement.

Why Do You Think They Took Such An Interest In You?

It's their nature to be kind. One of the fundamental *mitzvahs* in the Torah is to live for, and empathize with, others. Jews who have been observant their entire lives ("FFB"), have not personally experienced the difficulties that we "searchers" have encountered. However, I think most of them have a much better idea of our struggle than we give them credit for. Even though I made the correct decision about not spending that Pesach with my family, I had tears in my eyes for most of the first hour of prayer on the eve of Pesach. I do not think many FFB's can say that they have been through that kind of experience even once, much less as many times as I have. But my *Rebbe*, his family and many of the other men I pray with knew that I was going through a tough time and were very supportive.

What About Dealing With Challenges Outside Of Becoming More Observant?

One in particular comes to mind. After Hurricane Andrew struck Miami and turned my life upside down, I moved back to Cleveland and lived with my parents while I looked for a place to live. Once I found a place, I sent for my household belongings that had been in storage in Florida. When the movers arrived, they opened the door to the moving van. I was stunned. Everything, and I do mean *everything* I owned was ruined. The storage facility had not adequately repaired a leak from Hurricane Andrew and water from another storm had dripped onto all of my belongings. In the entire storage facility, my belongings were the only ones that were ruined. At first, I was hurt and mad. In retrospect, however, there were a variety of benefits. It helped me "start over." When I decided to move to an apartment near Telshe Yeshiva, I had very few belongings to move. It helped me see the fallacy of being attached to material goods.

What Has Kept You Going?

Hashem, **my** *Rebbe* **and a different attitude.** We don't get challenges we can't handle. So a couple of times when life became really difficult, I think *Hashem* just stepped in and said, "He's had enough." Also, I couldn't have done it without the support and encouragement of my R*ebbe* and my family. That's for sure. Most importantly, I decided that taking on *mitzvahs* would improve the quality of my life in *this* world.

Can You Suggest Anything A Little More Concrete?

I'll try. First, take pride in your accomplishments. Keep a list of each *mitzvah* you take on, including the prohibited activities that you give up. Second, internalize the advantages of being observant. Look at the beauty of the relationships between observant husbands and wives, and decide that there is only one way to obtain that closeness. Look at their children, and realize that you can only turn out kids that special in an observant household. Observe what it means to live in a community where keeping up with the Joneses revolves around how learned you are, instead of what kind of car you drive. In short, you have to set and achieve goals that bring about benefits that are truly central to our happiness.

What Else Should I Be On The Lookout For?

Don't put yourself in a position to be tested. If you're allergic to chocolate, why take a job in a candy shop? I have enough difficulty conquering challenges that *Hashem* puts in front of me. I see no reason to inflict additional challenges upon myself. For instance, I don't go into restaurants that

Step Seven: Recognize Challenges as Opportunities to Grow

are not kosher with a bunch of friends who are going to have a six-course meal I'd otherwise like to eat. Our environment affects us all, especially if it's an environment that we were once a part of.

Do You Ever Regret Taking On A Challenge?

No. That would be like regretting that someone did me a favor. Perhaps the challenges sometimes come a little too often, or are more intense than I'd like, but I can honestly say that I always look back on them and appreciate having gone through them. We all naturally want to do the right thing, but to allow us to grow and gain credit for our decisions; *Hashem* gives us the opportunity to follow the wrong path. The upside is, each time we make the right decision we are rewarded. The downside is that we are constantly faced with opportunities to make a poor decision and reduce the pleasures of being Jewish.

How Do You Resist Going Down The Wrong Path?

Don't laugh. The more you study Torah and the more *mitzvahs* you take on, the easier it is to make the right decisions. I used to think this was just a function of the fact that the more I learned, the more guilty I felt when I did something wrong. But it's more than that. Learning and *mitzvahs* don't just make us feel guilty about doing something we shouldn't; they actually reduce our desire to do the wrong thing. Keep in mind, though, that as you become more observant, the challenges get more sophisticated.

How Does That Work?

Once you have mastered a particular skill, you don't continue to view it as a challenge. In the first grade, the alphabet is a challenge. In the second grade, addition and subtraction are a challenge, but not the alphabet. In the third grade, multiplication is a challenge, but not addition, subtraction or the alphabet. Someone (like me, for instance) who has been keeping *Shabbos* for a couple of years might not be tempted to drive on *Shabbos*, but might have a hard time committing to learn *Gemara* on a consistent basis. The tricky part is getting past the "early stage" of each challenge.

Those FFB's (observant since birth) Really Have It Easy.

They wouldn't agree. In a certain sense, FFB's have more difficult challenges than we do, because we have experienced the secular lifestyle in all its glory, and we know the "grass isn't greener on the other side." We made a choice to become observant that was relatively easy because we knew the benefits and drawbacks of both a secular lifestyle and an observant lifestyle. It's more difficult for FFB's to withstand the allure of secularism and the "grass is always greener " mentality, because they have always been observant.

Doesn't It Drive You Crazy To Constantly Be On Guard?

You get over it. I started out being incredibly excited about the benefits of an observant lifestyle. Then, for about two months, I felt as if I was walking on eggshells.

You could see the distress on my face as I realized that there were consequences to everything I said and did. I got flack from people who said, "You used to enjoy life so much, and now that you're becoming more Jewish, you seem so depressed." Getting through that period is one of the biggest tests any of us will face, because we don't foresee the end of it. I am willing to bet that many of us drop out after the initial euphoria of being exposed to Torah observance has given way to the realization of the task ahead. We get discouraged, slide back into some old habits, and then it's over. If we had stuck with the program just a little longer, we would realize how much our lives have improved.

There Are Hurdles In All Learning.

Exactly. Imagine that the answers to accomplishing all of our goals were in an envelope on the top floor of a 120-story building. When we arrive, the doorman points us to the stairs. Some of us would give up right there because we perceived the climb as too difficult, while others would give up after a few floors. But some of us keep going. The climb becomes increasingly difficult, especially when we hear the voices below of those who quit, calling out, "Come back down and take it easy." But then we reach the 30th floor—where there is an express elevator to the top floor. That is what becoming more observant is all about. It looks difficult before we start. It is difficult as we get into the process. But we eventually get to the 30th floor.

What's The Key To Getting To The 30th Floor?

Understanding the incredible benefits of being Torah observant. And having the confidence that we can obtain and maintain Torah observance. To give us the strength to make it all the way, it's best to spend as much time as possible around observant Jews to appreciate how fulfilling their lives are.

Now That You Have Worked Out The Kinks With Your Family, What's Your Most Difficult Challenge?

You mean challenges.

Ego. I had a certain image of myself, and I wanted people to think of me in that manner. I was constantly worrying what people would think when they heard I observed *Shabbos* or was keeping kosher or living by a *yeshiva.* Worst of all, what would people think or say when they saw me wearing my *yarmulka?* I am trying to train myself to make decisions based on what *Hashem* would think of my behavior, not on what other people think.

Stress. It's easy to slide back into old habits when I am under a lot of pressure. I have spoken to a number of people who have traveled a similar path and they all agree that this is a problem. It doesn't matter if the stress is related to work, family, financial considerations, sickness or something more mundane. The key is to mentally prepare yourself so you can control your reactions to stressful situations, and not deal with stress in an unproductive manner.

Travel. When I am in my element, I am fairly consistent about my observance. But when I travel, I seem to forget or ignore certain aspects of my observance that I thought were second nature. I really have to be on guard.

Making time to learn. Not to just learn the weekly Torah portion, which I enjoy, but committing myself to learning *Gemara*, which is a struggle because of my poor Hebrew skills.

Being consistent.

I Think I Need A List Of Suggestions For Dealing With Challenges
Here goes.

1. Realize that all challenges are opportunities to grow and learn.

2. Each time you have a challenge, try to analyze why you are being faced with that particular challenge.

3. Take some positive action in response to each challenge; even if you are not 100% sure it is the right course of action.

4. Don't look for challenges ... they'll find you!

5. Concentrate on the benefits of being observant so you will have goals which will offer alternatives to behavior that might otherwise sidetrack you.

6. If the challenge comes because your family has to alter their behavior because of your growth, spend some time explaining what you are trying to accomplish and give them some time to get used to the idea. You didn't become observant overnight, and you can't expect them to adapt to your changes any faster than you took them on.

7   Be patient.

8. Don't be afraid to ask for help.

9. Don't give up.

10. Trust that *Hashem* has your best interests at heart.

From FEAR to ETERNITY

Step Eight

The Other Side
Of The Coin

Step 8: Examine The Other Side Of The Coin

One of the most difficult concepts to come to grips with in the process of becoming more observant is that not only are many secular teachings different than the Torah's view, but they are exactly the opposite of what the Torah teaches us. The following few examples highlight how we have to re-train the way we process information.

Sticks and stones may break my bones, but names will never hurt me.

On the contrary: broken bones heal, but our words can permanently injure someone. An inadvertent phrase can prevent a marriage, or ruin a perfectly fine business arrangement. In addition, physical violence has an adverse effect only on the person to whom it is directed. Speaking *loshon hora*—slander, gossip, and other forms of inappropriate speech—adversely affects three people: the person who is speaking; the person who hears the *loshon hora*; and the person who is being spoken about. The Torah prohibition against gossiping is so strong that we are taught to refrain from praising people in certain situations because it may induce someone to shout out a rebuttal. For instance, someone saying, "Adam is such a nice fellow," could lead another person to respond, "Yes, but did you know that he...."

Happy New Year. Observant Jews consider Rosh Hashana to be the day *Hashem* judges us on how we behaved during the previous year, and determines what we will encounter next year. We coronate *Hashem* as King, pause for an introspective look at the previous year, and make a solemn request that we be given another year of life in which to fulfill our goals. Contrast this with January 1ˢᵗ.

There were no Jewish heroes in the Holocaust. Because of the great pain involved, many Holocaust survivors were unable, until recently, to recount the miraculous stories of survival and heroic actions of defiance that were so commonplace during the reign of terror perpetrated by the Nazis (may their names be erased). Now, however, every Jewish bookstore has dozens of these stories. For a graphic reminder of the heroic nature of individuals who lived through the Holocaust, go into a *shul* during morning prayer services. When the men are putting on their *tefillin*, look for an elderly man with concentration camp numbers tattooed on his forearm. Anyone who came through that experience with his beliefs still intact is a hero by anyone's standards.

As we evolve, we are improving. Secularists believe that we crawled out of the sludge, progressed to walking on all four legs, progressed to being ape-like, and ultimately, progressed to being able to make popcorn in a microwave. We believe that *Hashem* created Adam, a perfect man, and the further we get from him, the less perfect we become. In addition, we believe that the further we get from the acceptance of the Torah at Mount Sinai, the further we are from our forefathers, who were on the highest possible spiritual level. Although they didn't have e-mail, they did have a society that held itself to the highest code of ethical conduct: the Torah. If you don't think our society is regressing in regards to our moral/ethical standards, ask your grandparents how people treated each other when they were growing up.

Let's kill a few hours. We all need downtime to re-charge our batteries, but the Torah tells us that "just killing time" is a tragedy of epic proportions. If you were to ask someone who was dying whether they would trade $100 for an extra day of life, they would jump at the chance. But how often do we waste an hour, a day, or cumulatively, a week, a month, or a year?

Don't get married until you can afford it. The *mitzvahs* of marrying and starting a family are not based on net worth. We believe that *Hashem* identifies your *bashert*, the person who is destined to be your mate, be-fore you are born, and that before you get married you will meet your *bashert*. But what if you meet your *bashert* when you're not in a financial position to have a wedding for all of your relatives and friends, and then set up a house-hold? Marriage is a *mitzvah*. It has to take place, notwithstanding financial considerations. So the observant community is sometimes called upon to help. Having chil-dren is also a *mitzvah*, and when times are tough, the observant community is there again to be called upon.

The most worthy charities raise the most money and are the most well-known. There is an incredible reward awaiting those individuals who give charity to in-dividuals and institutions that further the ideals set forth in the Torah. Unfortunately, until recently, I had never heard the names of these charities, much less the important func-tions that they perform.

If we have too many children, our quality of life will suffer. I have lots of friends with between one and three kids who seem to have a very nice life. I also have quite a few friends with four or more kids. I can't help but feel that the lives of the latter are more fulfilling than those of the former. They might not drive cars that are as flashy or live in houses that are as spacious, but they seem to have a more joyous existence. More children lead to more grandchildren. More *bar mitzvahs*, more weddings, more of everything that gives meaning to our lives.

It's Passover. We're free. The concept bantered about at most Pesach Seders is that *Hashem* freed us from the bondage of slavery, and we are now free to do whatever we want, whenever we want. What most of us don't realize is that *Hashem* freed us from Pharaoh's yoke so we could live according to the Torah. It isn't a coincidence that the Pesach story of the Jewish people leaving Egypt immediately precedes the events of Mount Sinai, where we accepted the Torah.

From FEAR *to* ETERNITY

Step Nine

Be A Mensch

Step 9: Be A Mensch

My *Rebbe* once met with a wealthy couple who did not believe in *mitzvahs*. They did, however, feel they were *mensch*es of the highest order.

So he asked them, "Do you ever visit fellow Jews who are confined to hospitals or nursing homes?" They replied that they felt uncomfortable around sick people.

"Have you ever helped out a young couple who wanted to get married with the expenses of their wedding or setting up their household?" They replied that if a couple didn't have enough money to pay for a wedding, they shouldn't get married.

"Have you ever taken people into your home who needed a place to stay for a night?" They replied that they lived in such a nice home, they couldn't risk having their valuables taken.

So my *Rebbe* said, "Then you must surely make charitable donations."

"Yes, naturally we do."

"Do you give 50% of your income?" he challenged

"Of course not," she replied.

"How about 40%?"

"Not even close," was the response.

"How about 20%?"

"No."

"How about 10%?"

"No."

"5%?"

The women thought for a minute, then asked her husband, "What do you think, honey, around 2%?"

And that's where they settled.

What Is A Mensch?

Literally, it is defined as a "man." However, we typically use it to describe a person of good character. More specifically, it is a person who exemplifies the qualities that *Hashem* says are important.

So Why Did The People In The Story Think They Were *Mensches*?

Because they weren't hurting anyone. But that is not enough. As Jews, so much more is expected of us. In today's vernacular, we have to be *pro-active*. To remind us how important it is to be a *mensch*, we recite a portion of the *Talmud* every morning which sets forth some of the prerequisites for being a *mensch*.

Do We Really Have To Give 50% Of Our Income To Charity?

The Torah says 10%. The truth of the matter is that *Hashem* provides each of us with all of our needs. Mandating that we give a portion of our income to charity is Hashem's way of giving us a chance to perform an act of kindness that He would perform anyway. Like any other *mitzvah*, our sages have established guidelines for us to follow. First, we should have the right intent when we give, having in mind that we're fulfilling a Torah *mitzvah*. If we're going to give anyway, we do so with joy in our hearts, not grudgingly. Not because it makes us feel good, but because we are seizing an opportunity to share something that *Hashem* gave us. Although it is not always possible, there is a preference for giving anonymously. It's also probably better to donate funds without requiring the recipient to put our names on the side of a building, unless we have some particularly worthy motivation such as inspiring others to make a similar donation. We should also recognize that some charities are more worthy than others. Just writing a check to a non-profit organization does not constitute charity from a Torah perspective. Since we believe that this world would not exist for even one moment unless Torah was being studied, assisting Torah scholars must be given a high priority. Ask your rabbi/*rebbe* for suggestions.

What Do I Get For My Money?

More than you think. Generally, we can't test *Hashem*. We can't say, for example, "*Hashem*, I'll study an extra hour of Torah every Wednesday night this month, and you help me get an A on my calculus exam." The one exception is charity. The more we give, the more we get back.

Some Months Are A Little Tight.

No problem. Give what you can and commit to make up the difference in the future. Say you should give $300 and you can only manage $250. You can give the other $50 when it becomes available to you.

Some Months Are REALLY Tight.

Lucky thing you're Jewish. Most observant communities have at least one free loan society. These societies make interest free loans and don't require you to put up your house or your first-born son as collateral. Many of these societies lend out millions of dollars each year.

Inviting Strangers Into Your Home Is Part Of Being A Mensch?

That's what the Torah says. For various reasons, I have found myself needing a place to stay for *Shabbos* in a number of cities. My *Rebbe* would usually arrange for me to stay at the home of someone I had never met. Shortly before *Shabbos*, my hosts would welcome me, show me to my room and give me a key to their house. I would then go to pray in a *shul* where I didn't know a soul. On more than one occasion there was almost a race between certain members of the *shul* to invite me to their homes for a meal. I would always be offered another home to stay in the next time I visited that neighborhood.

Once, while walking back to the home of the family with whom I was staying after the evening prayers at the conclusion of *Shabbos*, I heard a man screaming, "*Gut vach, gut vach* (good week, good week)," the traditional greeting for the night after *Shabbos*. He was running toward me at such a pace that he had to hold his hat in place to keep it from flying off his head. He introduced himself and told me that he had heard that a guest was in the community, and he wanted to make sure that the next time I came, I would stay with him and his family. He had no idea who I was, yet he was running after me to perform the *mitzvah* of inviting a guest to one's home.

What if I Show Up At A Shul On Shabbos And No One Offers Me A Place To Eat?

Just ask the rabbi for a recommendation. Although it helps to call ahead of time and say that you plan on being in the community.

I Don't Know If I Could Stay In The Home Of Someone I Didn't Know

I felt the same way. We don't feel comfortable about staying in the home of a complete stranger, because we wouldn't feel comfortable about having a complete stranger stay with us. I definitely felt that way when I first started staying at my *Rebbe's* home every *Shabbos*. But then I began to see the beauty of having guests who are strangers. There is a wonderful feeling that comes from providing for the needs of people you barely know. I know it pleases my *Rebbe* and his wife to no end when a guest in their home asks for something unusual to eat or drink which they can provide.

There is something else I have noticed about this *mitzvah*. The children in the homes who customarily have guests always look forward to it. Given the demanding schedules of most observant Jews, you would think their children would want to spend *Shabbos* alone with their parents, to have all of the *Shabbos* table's attention directed toward them. Instead, these children are disappointed if their families don't have guests at every meal on every *Shabbos*. By having guests in their home, children come to love their fellow Jews, irrespective of their level of observance.

Having Guests Is One Thing, But Visiting Strangers In A Hospital? Come On Now.

No, you come on. Imagine how someone would feel if they were confined to a hospital or nursing home for an extended period of time. After a while their friends would surely tire of visiting on a regular basis. Then, suddenly they are being visited by complete strangers who show a sincere interest in their well-being. These *strangers* spend a few dollars and bring them a couple of magazines or a kosher snack. Don't you think that would brighten up their day? Don't you think they'd look forward to the next visit?

Does Anyone Actually Do That?

If you're ever in the hospital near an observant community, remember these words: *Bikur Cholim*. Observant Jews will be coming out of the woodwork to ask if you'd like a refrigerator in your room or if there is any special food you'd like. They will try to bring you whatever you want to read. They will sit and talk to you. If your relatives are coming to town to visit you, they will try to find a place for them to stay. And in New York, the largest and most efficient private ambulance service is run by observant Jews.

Can't I Start By Visiting Someone I Know?

Absolutely. Recently, I went to visit an elderly woman who was housebound. When I arrived, I found that she had put on her finest clothes, made me tea and put out some homemade cookies. Her entire day had been uplifted by my short visit. Not just the hour or so I was there, but also the time she needed to prepare for my visit and, I am sure, the time after I left, when she meticulously cleaned up.

What About Being A Mensch On A Day-To-Day Basis?

There are a lot of opportunities. There is a famous story about Rabbi Moshe Feinstein, one of the truly righteous people of this century. He was typically surrounded by Torah scholars wherever he went, but on one occasion an ordinary fellow was given the honor of driving Reb Moshe to an appointment. When he helped Reb Moshe into the car, he slammed the car door on Reb Moshe's hand. As the man walked around the back of the car to get into the driver's seat, Reb Moshe quietly opened the car door to free his hand. When Reb Moshe got home, his son noticed that his father's hand was bleeding. He asked his father why he hadn't cried out, or at least mentioned it, so that ice could be applied or the wound could be cleaned. Reb Moshe's response: "Can you imagine the embarrassment that the driver would have felt if he had known that he had hurt me!"

I'm Not On That Level.

Neither am I. But life does present opportunities. My *rebbe* once gave a class on the topic of being a *mensch* and used the example of the correct response when a stranger asks if you have change for a $10 bill. Without looking, most people usually answer, "No." He suggested trying the opposite response—to immediately say, "Yes," and then look to see if you have the change. A couple of weeks later on a Sunday night, I was at the airport check-in counter trying to change a ticket. I was supposed to have left the night before, after *Shabbos* was over, which would have given me the all-important "Saturday night stay." Since I would no longer have a trip that extended over a Saturday night, I should have been charged an additional $375. In the middle of the transaction, an elderly black man asked me if I had change for a $20. I immediately said, "Yes," not knowing if I did or I didn't. I pulled out my wallet and by chance I was able to break his $20. I then turned back to the ticket agent, who completed changing my ticket. Not only hadn't she charged me the $375, she didn't even charge me the customary $50 which is normally required for changing any ticket.

Unfortunately, we don't learn about how to be a *mensch* in every specific situation that confronts us, but adopting a "do unto others ..." philosophy would certainly be a start.

Any Other Thoughts On Being A Mensch?

It takes work. You have to train yourself to look for ways to do kindness to others. I was lucky that one time at the airport because my *rebbe* had prepared me for that exact situation. It's much harder when you are under pressure at work, or you're tired, or you're coming down with a cold. Another situation we all deal with is when someone criticizes our new dedication to *mitzvahs*. I have had to train myself to respond with a question instead of a witty retort ... to ask why they perceive a situation a certain way ... or better yet, not to say anything at all.

Such was the case at a recent dinner when a guest mentioned, for my benefit, that a certain observant Jew was getting a divorce. More than a few people at the table turned to look at me. They were waiting for me to call out the divorce statistics from the guest's temple or to inquire about the statistics in his own family. I said nothing, and avoided embarrassing a fellow Jew, even though that was his intention toward me.

From FEAR to ETERNITY

Step Ten

Love Your Neighbor

Step 10: Love Your Neighbor

This morning when I opened the front door to pick up my newspaper, a headlined blared, *"CIA Veteran Accused of Espionage."* I reacted how I usually do when I hear a story about someone flouting the law in such a public way: "I hope he's not Jewish!" (thank G-d he wasn't). I have always responded this way, and when I quizzed my friends and family, I found that my feelings weren't so unusual.

Why Is That?

I don't know. It just seems that notwithstanding all the differences between us, on some level we all feel responsible for one another. Perhaps it is a holdover from our collective acceptance of the Torah at Mount Sinai. Perhaps it's been ingrained in our genetic make-up. Perhaps it's an "us against them" mentality. Perhaps it comes from going through the Holocaust and other atrocious periods of anti-Semitism.

Then Why Do Observant Jews Have a Holier-Than-Thou Attitude Toward Non-Observant Jews?

They shouldn't, and generally don't. But have you ever tried to explain a very simple concept to someone who just doesn't get it? After a while, you get a little frustrated. Soon your reasoned explanation takes on the tone of a lecture from the high and mighty. It's conceivable you could even say something sarcastic. Observant Jews wish all Jews could experience the incredible benefits of observing the Torah. They wish that we would all seize the benefits of a close relationship with *Hashem* that is there for the asking. They wish that so many Jews wouldn't go through the pain of intermarriage or divorce. On some level, it scares them that a Jew could go through an entire lifetime without observing one *Shabbos* or putting on *tefillin*. Perhaps they feel guilty that they receive incredible benefits from being observant and so many Jews don't. For those Jews who do have a holier-than-thou attitude, see "Ten More Practical Tips - Item 7."

But They Make Me Feel…..

I doubt it. If you were sitting around with a bunch of doctors and they didn't ask you your opinion, you might start to feel a little inadequate. It's not something they said, but the way you feel based on being around people who have greater knowledge of a particular subject than you do.

But They Are So Judgmental.

Not in the way you think. We are obligated to view other Jews with the greatest possible merit. We must give everyone the benefit of the doubt. If we see someone we know to be scrupulously honest withdrawing his hand from an unattended cash register, we are obligated to interpret it in a positive way—perhaps he is getting change from a larger bill he already put in. If you're Jewish, you're Jewish, and no Jew in his right mind would deny it. Similarly, if you're a *mensch*, you will be respected as a *mensch*.

But I Don't Think They Respect My Commitment To Being Jewish

What is your commitment? With the help of a Jewish mother who is an AAD (Almost A Doctor), I can get through most minor illnesses without too much official medical help. But how do you think a doctor would react if I asked him to respect me as a surgeon? I didn't go to medical school. I wasn't an intern or a resident. I don't practice medicine on a daily basis. If you want observant Jews to accept you for being *as Jewish* as they are, then you have to put in the same amount of time and effort in being Jewish as they do.

Why Can't They Just Leave Me Alone?

I'll tell you why. If there is one *mitzvah* that every non-observant Jew embraces, it's "Love your neighbor as you love yourself." But look at that commandment from the perspective of an observant Jew. If you walked into your home and saw your child with a bottle of poison in her hand and she was getting ready to take a drink, you'd start yelling and screaming to get her attention. You'd run over to her and forcibly knock the bottle out of her hands. You would admonish her to never do that again. Just to be sure, you'd put that bottle in a place she could never reach. Observant Jews look at the failure to observe the *mitzvahs* set forth in the Torah as being exponentially worse than drinking poison. Someone who drinks poison loses his or her life. Someone who does not observe *mitzvahs* may be jeopardizing their eternity.

It's My Life.

Let me put it another way. If you bought the winning lottery ticket and forgot about it, wouldn't you want someone to remind you?

But...

Let me put it to you another way. We Jews are all in the same boat. If one us decides to drill a hole in the bottom of the boat, he can't just say, "Hey, I bought this seat and if I want to cool off my feet with a little salt water, it's none of your business."

But...

Mazel Tov. At some point an observant Jew will break into a big smile and extend a heartfelt "Mazel tov," and you will have no idea what he is talking about. He will see your blank expression and inform you that his daughter just got engaged or he became a grandfather or some other joyous news. He is reinforcing his belief that we are all connected. That his joy is our joy. That we should be as happy about his *simcha* (joyous event) as we would be about our own.

What About The Observant Jew Who Steals Or Lies Or Cheats?

No observant Jew thinks it's okay to steal or lie or cheat. He does it in spite of his observance, not because of it. No one is perfect. He's not observant in that area. And he knows it. *Hashem* judges us as individuals and according to our own abilities. An observant Jew knows that committing a sin has consequences in this world and in the World to Come. Most non-observant Jews do not have a well-defined concept of how life-death-judgment-reward-punishment and eternity are interrelated. So when most people do something wrong and get away with it, they think they have really gotten away with it, or worse, that the act was permissible. An observant Jew does not labor under that mistaken belief.

But How Do They Justify Doing Things That Are Blatantly Wrong?

They don't. You have to appreciate that we all have challenges and we all make mistakes. However, someone else's misdeeds do not justify our own. We can't say that an observant Jew doing something wrong gives us license to drive to *shul* on *Shabbos* or to eat pork fried rice.

Observant Jews Stay Married Because They Have No Choice.

Wrong again. Divorce exists in the observant community, but in infinitesimally smaller numbers than in the secular Jewish community and society as a whole. The question is, "Why?" It's obviously beyond the scope of this book, but I don't think it is a function of one particular factor. True, observant Jews do tend to get married young and thus establish bonds that are the result of experiencing aspects of life for the first time together. They also try to start a family right away, which establishes a common purpose for getting up in the morning. They also have fewer day-to-day issues to deal with because they have clearly defined goals. They know they are going to keep kosher and observe *Shabbos* and send their kids to Jewish schools and live according to the other *mitzvahs* in the Torah. When they hit a rough spot, as all marriages do from time to time, they have an incredible support system in the Torah, as well as rabbis to turn to for direction.

And They All Live So Simply

That's not necessarily a negative, and not necessarily true. As most people will tell you, their headaches increase as their possessions increase. Just ask anyone who has a vacation home. By and large, observant Jews do not define themselves by what they do for a living, and thus do not call attention to themselves through their possessions or their jobs. Accordingly, many extremely wealthy observant Jews tend to live more conservatively than non-observant Jews with the same net worth. Everyone knows they need to make a certain amount of money to support a family, but beyond the effort needed to earn that amount, observant Jews are under no pressure to put in the extra hours at work to climb the corporate ladder. If anything, the pressure is quite the opposite. By the way, anyone who has toured Deal, New Jersey; Monsey, New York; Hancock Park, California; or Lawrence, New York would not accuse the observant residents of living simply.

Why Do The Men All Dress Alike?

They're in uniform. Military personnel have a certain bearing that lets you know that they are proud to be in their particular branch of the service. Observant Jewish men wear different types of head coverings, including their black hats, and non-flamboyant clothing proudly, because they are in *Hashem's* army.

Why Do The Women Dress In Such Plain Outfits?

Not all of them do. Observant women run the same gamut as secular women. Some look like they stepped right out of Vogue magazine, and others dress more simply. But, yes, they do observe the laws of *tznius*—modesty—that discourages a woman from wearing seductive clothing that calls attention to them for the wrong reason. If they are going to be the center of attention, they prefer that it be because of their learning or their intellect or their accomplishments. It is an approach that is in keeping with the feminist ideal of judging a woman by her accomplishments, not by her appearance. In addition, there is a concept that women should dress up for their husbands, not for the world at large. Accordingly, they put on their best outfits on *Shabbos* and other holidays when their families are around, not when they go to work or to the store.

But You Have To Admit That In General, All Observant Jews Are Pretty Much Alike.

Just the opposite. Jews can be divided into two basic groups: Sephardic Jews who originated from Spain and certain countries in the Middle East; and Ashkenazic Jews who originated from Eastern Europe. Whether they are Sephardic or Ashkenazic, in terms of the customs they follow, most reform Jews practice Judaism like all other reform Jews, and most conservative Jews practice Judaism like all other conservative Jews. Not so with observant Jews. Within the community of observant Sephardim, the Jews from Syrian, Morocco, Yemen and other Middle Eastern countries each have different customs. Within the Ashkenazic community, there are Chassidic Jews and Jews who generally trace their customs back to the Lithuanian Jewish community. The Chassidic Jews generally have a *rebbe* whom the entire community follows, such as the Lubavitcher Rebbe or the Gerrer Rebbe or the Satmar Rebbe, who are named for the towns from which they descended. They typically wear long black coats, have pronounced earlocks, long beards, and wear unique fur hats. What most of us consider the traditional orthodox community descends from the great yeshivas of Eastern Europe such as Volozhin, Telshe, Slobodka and Mir. Within these communities, there are *yeshivish* Jews and modern orthodox Jews—and a lot of Jews in between.

My Sister Wants To Ask You A Few Questions.
Shoot.

Why Do Orthodox Jews Treat Women As Second Class Citizens?

They don't. Let's start with the proposition that *Hashem* doesn't make mistakes. That He made men and women different just happens to be a fact that we have to deal with. Could He have made us exactly the same? Of course. The fact that He didn't, must mean there are some basic differences, including the obligations that *Hashem* very clearly gave us.

You're Going With A Separate But Equal Argument?

No, equal but different. Neither gender is superior. They have different functions.

If We Are So Equal, How Come We Can't Sit Next To You When We Pray?

It's not what you think. Prayer is the primary way in which we communicate with *Hashem*. The fact of the matter is that men can't concentrate on prayer when they are in close proximity to women. I used to think this was bunk, but it is a fact of life. For close to a year I never saw a woman when I was praying. I then happened to be in a *shul* in which the women were in a balcony that wrapped around. If you tried, you could see the women. Unfortunately, many of us sitting in the men's section did just that.

Why Can't I Give My Orthodox Friends Of the Opposite Sex A Hug?

Familiarity breeds familiarity. Our Sages teach us that casual contact between the sexes starts with desires that are the result of seeing something that is forbidden, but available. Thus, our rules about dressing modestly. After seeing something we desire, the next step is to touch it, and from there, who knows. I know the argument. What's a handshake? Does a little kiss on the cheek really matter? In most cases you might be right, but why take a chance?

Why Aren't Women Obligated To Pray Three Times Per Day?

It's a time bound *mitzvah.* Women are exempt from many positive *mitzvahs* that must be done at a certain time of the day. Prayer is one such *mitzvah* because it must be done before a certain time in the morning, at certain times in the afternoon, and after sunset. The exemption is in recognition of the fact that a woman's primary obligation is to provide an environment in the home which is conducive to a Jewish family, and that many of those obligations occur at unpredictable times.

That is not to say that women are exempt from prayer, because they aren't. It's just that they are not obligated to do so at a particular time and in a particular place. Women are, however, subject to all of the negative *mitzvahs*, and can voluntarily perform most positive *mitzvahs*.

What If I Want To Work?

Knock yourself out. There is nothing in the Torah that prevents a woman from working. If she has the time and the inclination to work, there is no prohibition that I know of. My *Rebbe* and his wife have 12 kids ranging in age from 1 to 18. His wife still finds time to teach a few days each week, organize a charity auction and perform many other acts of kindness in the community.

Can You Explain The Concept Of A Woman Going To The Mikveh (ritual bath)?

It's beyond the scope of this book. But you might try reading *The Waters of Eden* by Aryeh Kaplan and *The Secret of Jewish Femininity* by Tehilla Abramov. Then I would suggest asking a Rebbitzen any questions you may have.

Can I Ask You A Personal Question?

As long as it's just between us.

Do You Think You're Better Than Me Just Because You've Become More Observant?

***Chas Vesholom* (G-d forbid).** What I do think is that *I* am a better person than *I* used to be. I have plenty of regrets about choices I made and how I treated certain people. I should have known better then, and I certainly know better now.

I can't compare myself to you or anybody else. I can only determine how my life has improved. How my relationships with family and friends have deepened. How I am more at peace. How my life has more meaning. I still have long a way to go. But for me, I am definitely on the right road, and headed in the right direction.

A Day In The Life

Catchy title.

Thanks. I was asked to write a chapter on what it's like to spend the day as an observant Jew. The problem is, I am married with kids, so my day is vastly different from someone who is single or married without children or, perhaps most importantly, a woman.

Give It A Shot.

OK. As soon as we are awake, before even getting out of bed, we recite the following: *I gratefully thank You O living and eternal King, for you have returned my soul within me with compassion. Abundant is your faithfulness.* We start out the day thanking *Hashem* for giving us another day.

After using the bathroom we say the following blessing: *Blessed are you Hashem our G-d, King of the Universe, Who fashioned man with wisdom and created within him many openings and many cavities. It is obvious and known before your Throne Of Glory that if but one of them were to be ruptured or but one of them were to be blocked, it would be impossible to survive and to stand before You. Blessed are You Hashem, Who heals all flesh and acts wondrously.* Anyone who has had one of the aforementioned openings or cavities ruptured or blocked can immediately relate to why we are supposed to say this prayer every time we go to the bathroom.

Are We Out Of The House Yet?

Yes. And on our way to shul. Our first obligation is to thank *Hashem* for every single aspect of our well-being. We acknowledge His kindness and that He is responsible for everything, from our ability to see to the clothes we have on. We beseech Him to keep us away from challenges, scorn, sin and evil in general. And of course, we thank Him for giving us the Torah.

OK, Let's Go To Work.

We're just getting started. Then we say the *Shema*, the first verse which we all know is, *"Hear O Israel, Hashem is our G-d, Hashem is the only One,"* and the three paragraphs that follow.

What Three Paragraphs?

The three paragraphs that focus our thoughts on the fact that Hashem is the Supreme Being. That He is the only one whose opinion we should be considering in our day-to-day lives. Then we say the *Amidah*, in which we beseech *Hashem* on our behalf, and on behalf of the entire world, that all of our needs should be met. We say all of these prayers while wearing *tefillin* on our arm to remind us that our physical strength is from, and for, *Hashem*, and on our head to remind us that our intellect is from, and for, *Hashem*. We also say all of these prayers while wearing *tzitzis*, which have 613 knots in them to remind us of the 613 *mitzvahs* that we are obligated to perform.

Can We Go To Work Now?

Sure, let's talk about approach. In the working world we are exposed to a variety of influences. Some good, some not so good, and some that are toxic. Our focus has to be that at the end of the day, we should feel as though we have lived life to the fullest. To do so, we have to arm ourselves for the battle against all of the non-kosher experiences that we may encounter.

We do that by praying. The morning prayers give us the strength to get to the afternoon, when we pray the afternoon prayers and again beseech *Hashem* to fulfill all of our needs in the *Amidah*. At some point, we go home to spend some quality time with our family, and hopefully, to spend some time learning Torah. In the evening we pray the evening prayers, where we again pray the *Amidah* and the *Shema*. When we are in bed and just before sleep, we say the bedtime *Shema*, in which we forgive anyone who has hurt us during the day and ask Hashem to grant us another day.

What Else Is Different For You On A Day-To-Day Basis?

Eating. I used to go out for lunch every day for an hour or so. Now, I typically eat at my desk. With kids and prayer and learning, my time is so short that to drive to a kosher restaurant, eat and drive back takes out too big a chunk of the day.

What About Business Lunches?

So far it hasn't been a big problem. Almost all big companies are extremely accommodating. If you tell them you keep kosher, they will order you a meal. If I find myself in a situation where I absolutely have to be in a non-kosher restaurant, I try to eat something before I go in so I won't be hungry. Of course, making *brachas* (blessings) at business meetings can lead to some explanations that are not central to the issues at hand, but it's not a big distraction.

What About All Of The Holidays?

And Shabbos. In the winter, when *Shabbos* can start before 5:00 PM, I have to leave work fairly early, but that is primarily a function of planning ahead. Similarly, when I have to miss a couple of days for a holiday, it's just a like a vacation day that anyone else might take, though with two important differences. When I practiced law, I was never sure I was on vacation until I got on the plane, because if an important project came up, I would occasionally have to cancel my plans. You can't cancel or postpone a Jewish holiday, and the people I work with have come to know that. Also, even when I was on vacation, I would occasionally get an emergency call that necessitated some work on my part. Since I don't use the phone on *Shabbos* or the holidays, that is no longer an option for my co-workers.

Anything Else That's Different?

Not really. Well, maybe. I wear a *yarmulka* and people I do business with are acutely aware that I am an observant Jew. So I feel some added pressure to treat people with respect, to not get angry and generally, to bend over backwards to be accommodating so as not to desecrate G-d's name.

Being On Guard Again.

It has more to do with being sensitive to what *Hashem* wants from us. And it's especially important in the business world. We come into contact with so many people, we have an almost unlimited number of opportunities to sanctify or desecrate *Hashem's* name. It requires us to be constantly aware of how *Hashem* wants us to conduct ourselves, especially when someone is rude or says something nasty about us.

How's It Going?

It's a work in progress.

Three Milestones

I. Your Rebbe

Where Were We?

We were trying to find you a *rebbe*.

Tell Me More About The Rebbe-Talmid Relationship.

The most important element: suspend your common sense. Common sense is the filtration system we use to make decisions. In other words, we filter a new experience through our accumulated experiences and decide how we should react. Unfortunately, growing up in the secular world has left us with a filtration system that typically filters out the Torah's view and leads us to reach decisions that are not in our best interests. Your *rebbe* is going to tell you things that don't square with your reality as it now exists.

I Like My View Of Reality.

That's the problem, it's your view. A king was once walking in a section of the forest where every tree had a white circle with an arrow stuck right in the bull's-eye. The king was amazed. "I'd like to meet the archer who could shoot with such remarkable accuracy," he thought to himself. Just then, he saw a nine-year-old boy shoot an arrow into a tree. The boy then took out a paintbrush and painted a circle around the arrow.

In a similar way, we typically get a gut feeling about something and then draw a circle around it. That is to say, if something feels good, it must be right. The Torah gives us a system that enables us to look at events from an objective viewpoint that has stood the test of time, instead of from a subjective viewpoint that is constantly changing.

Can You Give Me A Real Life Example Of Suspending Your Common Sense?

More than you can imagine. For those of us who used to work on *Shabbos*, it was impossible to believe that we could give up working on Saturdays and still make the same amount of money each year. But we did. For those of us on a budget with no room for error, it made no sense to give 10% of our income to charity. But we did and still had the same amount left over each month. None of us could imagine getting married without an extensive period of dating and pre-marital everything. But we met incredible mates, married and started wonderful families. The list goes on and on.

This is not to say that every challenge that you encounter will work out the way you want it to, especially right away. For some of us it seems impossible to make ends meet, while for others we just can't seem to get married or have children. See Step 7, "Recognize Challenges As Opportunities To Grow." But having a *rebbe* will certainly assist you in getting through these extremely difficult times.

Are There Any Other Keys To The Rebbe-Talmid Relationship?

Don't just listen to what your *rebbe* says, watch what he does. Watch how he encourages and disciplines his children and you will learn how to raise responsible adults. Watch how he holds his cup on Friday nights and you will learn the laws of making *Kiddish*, the prayer inaugurating *Shabbos* and holidays, which is said over a cup of wine. Take notes. Record every class. Come home after *Shabbos* and jot down everything that you can remember. *Rebbes* teach by example, as well as by what they say.

That Sounds Pretty Easy.

It is more challenging than you think. A new student once stayed at my *Rebbe's* home for *Shabbos*. His mother then asked him, "Is the rabbi orthodox?" He replied, "I don't know." So she asked, " Does his wife light candles on Friday night?" He thought for a minute and said, "I don't think so." In fact, at that time, there were 12 candles blazing away on my *Rebbe's* dining room table. (The custom of observant Jews is to light two candles, plus one candle for each child, shortly before *Shabbos* on Friday evening; my *Rebbe's* candles now number 14.) The point is, if you're not looking, you can miss even the most obvious signs.

What's The Most Unexpected Benefit Of Having A Rebbe?

In my experience: if you're single, finding a *shidduch* (marriage partner). If you're married, optimizing the marital relationship. Some substantial portion of a *rebbe's* waking hours are dedicated to finding *shidduchim* (a husband or wife, as the case may be) for his students. So the first benefit is accessing the network of likely mates. Second, your *rebbe* can save you a lot of time, expense and emotional turmoil by weeding out those individuals who are objectively not suitable for you, before you ever meet them. Third, your *rebbe* can help you with the difficult decisions that inevitably come up. Since all relationships go through stressful times, having a *rebbe* to help resolve disputes is an invaluable resource. According to the famous Torah Sage, Rabbi Avigdor Miller, one of the primary protections against divorce available to the observant community is having a *rebbe* whom you and your spouse trust, and to whom you can turn for advice.

Do I Have To Do Everything My Rebbe Tells Me To Do?

Unfortunately, no. Many of my most spirited discussions with my *Rebbe* centered on his suggesting that I take on a particular *mitzvah*, and me emphatically denying that I was ready. When I followed his advice, the process was quick and relatively painless. When I delayed, it was like taking a band-aid off a millimeter at a time, putting it back on and then ripping it off all over again. Outside of when and how to observe *mitzvahs*, my *Rebbe* rarely suggests a course of conduct unless I ask him a specific question. Since he has assisted a variety of people in maximizing the benefits of being Jewish, his advice is usually right on the mark. Although, of course, I don't always follow it.

Don't You Have A Mind Of Your Own Anymore?

I don't know, let me ask my *Rebbe*. You will know that you have a true *rebbe-talmid* (teacher–student) relationship when a friend or family member asks this question. They will perceive that you have lost all vestiges of free will. Since their only concept of someone who imparts knowledge is a teacher, they can't imagine the differences between a teacher and a *rebbe*. You can try to patiently explain those differences as I've tried to outline them in Step 2. You can also explain that you are still making your own decisions, but that the knowledge you have acquired is leading you to make different, and better, decisions than you made in the past. It won't be easy.

Why Should A Rabbi Agree To Become Your Rebbe?

There is no logical answer to this question. Let me start off by saying that my relationship with my *Rebbe* is quite unique. Not every *rebbe* will spend as much time with each of his students as mine did with me. Having said that, the fact remains that my *Rebbe* has invested thousands of hours in my development. I stayed in his home almost every *Shabbos* for six months. I then moved to an apartment within walking distance of his home, and for an additional twelve months I ate virtually all of my *Shabbos* meals in his home. We would often stay up until two or three o'clock in the morning, discussing the issues I couldn't resolve on my own (of which there were many). I, along with five or six other businessmen, learned *Gemara* with him six mornings each week in his home, where he often conducted classes. During Sukkos (eight days) and Pesach, also eight days, I ate almost every meal with my *Rebbe* and his family. I went to his classes every *Shabbos* afternoon, Tuesday evening, Thursday evening and Sunday morning. I talk to him about my business, about buying versus leasing a car, about my relationships with family and friends, about how to interpret current events from a Torah perspective and especially about the trials and tribulations of realizing the incredible benefits of being Jewish. I have shown up at his house at midnight to ask a question. I have called him from all over the United States to clarify a thought. He spoke to each woman I went out with, often for hours at a time, and to each of their rabbis or *rebbetzins.*

What Has He Gotten In Return?

You'd have to ask him. Since our sages liken the *rebbe-talmid* relationship to the father-son relationship, he has in essence expanded his family. I am sure he has a certain sense of accomplishment from having assisted me and so many other Jews in maximizing the benefits of being Jewish. I am also sure *Hashem* appreciates anyone who has such a dedicated love of his fellow Jews, especially those who didn't grow up observant. There are also some collateral advantages such as demonstrating to his children what it means "... to love your neighbor as yourself."

What Is The Greatest Impediment To Getting A Rebbe?

It's no surprise. Our own ego is the greatest impediment to allowing someone to teach us something that will change how we behave. Objectively looking at our lives, and critically examining the choices we are making is not an easy task.

I'm Not Sure I'm Ready To Change.

Then just keep taking classes and asking questions. You must put your *rebbe* in a position to assist you in changing how you look at every situation. You must allow your *rebbe* to show you how to view the world from the standpoint of doing *Hashem's* will, instead of your own. He won't be able to do that unless you're ready to change. I do not know what my *Rebbe* saw in me that motivated him to invest so much of his valuable time and resources in me, except that he was able to discern my willingness to grow. Not that I immediately took on every *mitzvah*. Far from it. But he knew that I had reached the conclusion that an observant lifestyle was, on every level, more rewarding than the alternative. He has had to use a variety of different motivational techniques to get me this far, and he has had to be extremely patient.

II. Dating and Marriage

What's New?

I got married.

WHAT! I Didn't Know You Were Even Dating.

It happened fairly quickly. A mutual friend fixed us up. We went out eight times over a few weeks and got engaged. The marriage took place about two and a half months later.

Fairly Quickly? How Could You Know Someone Well Enough After Eight Dates To Get Engaged?

Our dating was very focused. There was no pretense about intentions. All dating in observant circles is designed to lead to marriage. There were no questions about timing or waiting for certain events to occur. We, like all observant singles, wanted to get married and hopefully start a family as quickly as possible.

But There Are So Many Issues To Work Out.

Not as many as you think. Observant couples have fewer "issues" than non-observant couples. We know we are going to eat only kosher food, we know we are going to be observing Shabbos, and we know we are going to be sending our kids to Jewish day schools. We know an incredible amount about what our lives together are going to be like on a day-to-day basis. So it mostly comes down to chemistry and priorities.

So This Was One Of Those Pre-Arranged Marriages.

You have got to be kidding. We dated and made our own decisions, as do all observant Jews. It's just that what we were trying to determine—whether we had compatible goals—takes a lot less time than the issues that secular couples have to deal with.

But How Could You Fall In Love So Fast?

Lets define "love." You often hear people say they love to eat fish, or they love their new car. What they are really saying is that their "love" is based on the joy that something, or someone, is giving them. Similarly, we were raised by popular media to think that someone loves us based on how much they do for us.

Our view is quite the opposite. Love is generated by what we do for the other person. For instance, a mother who does nothing but feed, change and clothe an infant, loves that infant much more than the infant loves its mother. The definition of love that I am most comfortable with is the feeling one gets from making another person happy. Love is not a trivial part of observant marriages, but it comes over time and is based on what we do for our spouse, not on what our spouse does for us. You could love someone very much during the dating process, but if one of you wants to keep *Shabbos* and one doesn't, no amount of love or affection is going to solve that problem.

But How Did You Know...You Know.

A small leap of faith. All marriages require some leap of faith because one never knows what marriage will be like until it is experienced. Because our focus was not on physical chemistry, our dating emphasized the priority of establishing our spiritual and emotional chemistry. Which is not to say sparks didn't fly, because they did. But since our physical chemistry wasn't tested the way most couples do, you could argue that our leap of faith was a little broader.

Can I Ask You A Personal Question?
Sure.

Are You a Nerd?

I know what you're thinking. This guy couldn't get a date, so he finds a rabbi who will fix him up and then finds a girl who will marry him without pre-marital you-know-what. The fact is, most of my friends who were raised in the non-observant world and became observant are no different than you are. We played sports. We dated. We traveled. We went to college. We had and have choices. Most of us excelled in at least one area, which gave us the self-confidence to take on the challenges that resulted in our obtaining the benefits of becoming observant.

My *Rebbe's* current students are typical. One of us played football for a Big Ten School. One had a full music scholarship to a prestigious college and then went to a top law school. One is a respected surgeon.

What About The Women?

Let me tell you a story. When I was becoming religious, I kept asking my Rebbe if there were any religious women whom I would find attractive. I didn't mean spiritually and I didn't mean emotionally. I had never met any religious women so I had no idea what they looked like, what kind of families they came from, or what they did for a living. It was scary to think that I could end up observing all of these new laws by myself. So I went to the annual dinner of one of the organizations that works with educating Jewish women. I didn't meet my wife, but I was incredibly impressed. It was a group of women who were exactly like the women I had been exposed to my entire adult life. With one crucial difference: they had all made the same commitment to the Jewish religion that I had.

So I'll Find The Woman Of My Dreams?

You'll find your bashert. That is, you will meet the person with whom you were meant to spend the rest of your life. You will meet the person who will help you reach the goals that you have the ability to attain—and vice-versa. The issue is, will you be sensitive enough to realize who that person is, or will you fall into the BBD problem?

BBD?

Bigger, better deal. Always thinking that there is someone else out there who is better than the person you are with. It's the grass is greener mentality taken to its most illogical extreme.

It Sounds Pretty Difficult to Find Your Bashert.

Not really. We believe that Hashem will absolutely bring you together with your bashert before you get married. A man who had been dating for a long time complained to his rebbe about not finding his beshert. The rebbe told him, "She was the one you thought was too short." We have to have our spiritual antennas up or we may miss the signal.

There are a lot of wonderful Jewish women out there who are committed to having a Torah observant home. I have met nurses and teachers and lawyers. Women from every corner of the globe. Women in real estate and women in the arts. One of the women was an international award winning fashion designer who worked for Guess Jeans.

Tell Me About That Last One.

I married her. There are thousands of observant men and women in the United States alone who are bright and attractive and eligible and, most importantly, committed to getting the most out of life through their attachment to Torah and *mitzvahs.*

I Heard That Men and Women Don't Dance Together at Your Weddings.

That's not the only difference. Our weddings have to be seen to be appreciated. The joy is unmatched. And yes, the men dance with the men and the women with the women, but that only adds to the uniqueness of the event. However, the major difference is that the guests are obligated to entertain the bride and groom, not the other way around. Grandparents and small children alike join together to maximize the enjoyment of the bride and groom.

What About This Concept Of Not Being With Your Wife At Certain Times?

It's an unbelievable asset for observant couples. The Torah prescribes certain activities that are guaranteed to maximize chemistry in a marriage. For instance, there are certain times during the month that a man and woman are not allowed to touch each other, much less have marital relations. So the days immediately following and preceding these days of separation are exciting times. Contrast this with couples that can be affectionate any time they want. They don't appreciate not being able to be affectionate with their spouse so nothing drives them to be together. There is a little of "we all want what we can't have" and "absence makes the heart grow fonder" built into all observant marriages!

What Are The Days Like When You Can't Be Together?

Challenging—but rewarding. When we have a disagreement, we can't just hug each other and make up. We have to talk through issues and resolve them. It has made us much better at communicating and much more appreciative of being able to be affectionate.

III. Your First Child

I'm Afraid To Ask. Where've You Been This Time?

We just had our first child, *Baruch Hashem* (Thank G-d).

Mazel Tov.

Thank you. G-d willing, it should happen to you in the near future.

You Sure Didn't Waste Any Time ...

It depends on your perspective. I waited a long time to get married. I moved around, dated around and goofed around. Around and around I went.

Life Is Full Of Choices.

My point exactly. I have friends my age who have had kids for close to two decades. I think they made a great choice. They were young fathers, and will ultimately be young grandfathers. When the Torah says it's a *mitzvah* to get married and have children, it is telling us that they are amongst the best tools to achieve the most joy out of our too short existence.

How Did You Come Up With Your Son's Name?

It was a combination of factors. Our custom is to name our children after relatives who are deceased, lived long full lives, and had children, while Jews of Sephardic descent typically name their children after people who they want to honor who are still alive. We also name children after righteous individuals. With respect to our son's first name, we had in mind both my mother's father and Aharon, Moshe's brother, who was the leader of the Jewish people until Moshe returned to lead the Jews out of Egypt. With respect to our son's middle name, we had in mind both my mother-in-law's father and Yosef, Yaacov's son, who became the viceroy of Egypt. These ancestors, whose souls are still whirling about, will assist our son in his endeavors, while our son's *mitzvahs* will be an elevation of their souls.

That World To Come Connection Again.

You bet. We are not alone. In fact, every day in our prayers we start the central prayer, the silent *Amidah*, with a plea that Hashem should consider the merit of our forefathers Abraham, Isaac and Jacob in deciding how to deal with us. By naming our children after these and other righteous individuals, we are tightening up the connection.

Let's Get Back To This World. How Was The Bris?

Great. Our son was carried in like royalty on a white pillow. It's a special sign for him to be carried by friends who are seeking to have children (which they promptly did). He was placed on the lap of my *Rebbe* who held him during the *bris*, which is a special sign that he should grow in Torah and *mitzvahs*. Our family and many friends were there, and we ate a festive meal because it is also a *mitzvah* to break bread at a joyous event. It was done early in the morning just after morning prayers to indicate that we can't wait to do *mitzvahs*.

You Couldn't Wait To Circumcise Your Son.

I couldn't wait for him to enter into the Covenant of Abraham. You can have a Jewish mother or go through a kosher conversion and thus be Jewish. But there are special advantages of having a kosher circumcision. People who were circumcised in a hospital often have a kosher *bris* later in life when they realize what they are missing.

Conclusion

A man was constantly praying that he should win the lottery. Not just any lottery. A lottery that would forever satisfy all of his earthly wants and desires. Day after day, month after month, he prayed for the winning numbers. He cried. He stomped his feet and shook his fists.

One morning, after a number of years, he heard a heavenly voice calling to him: "Sam, BUY A TICKET."

I Know There Is A Point To This.

It's related to what makes Jews rich. For Jews, the "lottery," the key to satisfying all of our earthly and spiritual desires, is found in the Torah. Most of us need a rebbe to help us "pick the winning numbers," but that isn't such a great obstacle to overcome considering what we obtain in return.

You're Going To End This Book With A Joke.

No, three riddles. They are found in the fourth chapter of a must-read book, Pirkei Avos—the Ethics of the Fathers:

Who is wise? Who is strong? Who is rich?

Lets Work Backwards. Everybody Knows Who The Rich Are.

Not everybody. Let's say you have $10 million in the bank, which would be more than enough to support you and your family for the rest of your life. If your best friend were Bill Gates, you would most likely feel frustrated that you too couldn't build a $113 million dollar home. If your best friend were Ted Turner, you would no doubt be intimidated because you couldn't fly to your private island on your private jet. You would never feel "rich," much less satisfied.

In fact, the truly "rich" man is satisfied with what he has, no matter how much or how little. He doesn't covet the belongings of someone else because he realizes that whatever he has is exactly what *Hashem* wants him to have.

So, The Answer To "Who Is Wise" Isn't Albert Einstein?

You're a quick study. The simple answer is that one is "wise" if they learn from every person. A truly "wise" person will seek wisdom wherever it can be found, and will internalize it. That is, the wisdom they acquire will change them. For instance, you could go to a baseball game for its entertainment value. Or you can be "wise," and think about how tens of thousands of fans are deliriously excited to be sacrificing their time and money to attend an event that will have no lasting effect on them. You could use the reaction of the fans as motivation to use your time, money and excitement to attain goals that will improve your life on a daily basis.

That Leaves Us With "Who Is Strong."

That it does. Someone is "strong" if they can subdue their natural inclinations. Spiritual strength is the key to happiness—not having the ability to bench press your weight. When we subdue our natural inclination to get mad, or eat non-kosher food, or fall back to sleep instead of getting up to pray, or engage in one of the many, many acts that are difficult for us, we are strengthening ourselves so the next time we are faced with the same circumstances, we will more easily do the right thing.

This is illustrated in the verse that follows the question, "Who is strong?" "He who is slow to anger is better than the strong man." Anyone who has a bit of a temper will surely agree with that expression of strength.

So Where Does That Leave Us?

A final thought. Our greatest asset is our intellect. Unfortunately, we tend to use it primarily for self-preservation. Making a living, getting the kids to school on time, eating and the like. By attaching ourselves to the Torah and all that it has to offer, we can use our minds every single day to become wiser, stronger and richer. Imagine, if every day we became just a little wiser, a little stronger and a little richer, what would our lives would be like next year at this time.

Imagine How Wise, Strong And Rich We Could Be In 10 Years. Or How Much Better Our Relationships Could Be. Or How ...

I think you got it.

Ten Practical Tips

1. Find Yourself A Rabbi Who Will Be Your Rebbe

Yes, you've heard it before. See Step 2.

2. Keep An Open Mind

In the process of maximizing the benefits of being Jewish, we are exposed to many new concepts and novel ways of looking at our existing belief structure. Question everything you don't understand. Don't blindly follow the advice of others. But don't reject anything out of hand either. If you don't agree with something, don't assume that the concept isn't valid. If you aren't quite ready to take on a *mitzvah*, don't take the easy way out and decide you're never going to accept it upon yourself.

3. Get Out Of Your Comfort Zone

It would be great if we looked forward to taking on every *mitzvah* as soon as we heard about it. If we couldn't wait to get up every morning so we could be more observant. But that isn't reality for most of us. We have to extend ourselves to get what we want out of life. I could use the "no pain, no gain" analogy, but it is perhaps more apt to say "no effort, no results." Remember:

1. We get more "credit" for taking on a difficult *mitzvah* than an easy one.

2. *Hashem* doesn't give us tests we can't pass.

3. All we can do is make the effort; the results are up to *Hashem.*

4. Get Into Your Comfort Zone When You're Praying

First, you have to know what prayers to say. That can be accomplished fairly easily by sitting down with a rabbi who will walk you through the prayer book and mark the appropriate paragraphs.

Second, it's perfectly permissible to pray in English. As you get more comfortable, you will undoubtedly add more and more Hebrew. At some point you will find it strange to say any of the prayers in English, even if you don't know exactly what you are saying in Hebrew. As tough as Hebrew is to learn, it is that comfortable when you finally get it.

Third, being comfortable when you're praying is primarily a function of repetition. This is true not only with respect to reciting the actual prayers, but also in regard to the pacing, and knowing when certain prayers are added or deleted.

Fourth, be aware that the daily prayers are different on *Shabbos*, holidays and at the beginning of each new month.

5. Although Rome Wasn't Built In A Day, It Did Get Built.

The key to growth is to consistently move forward. It is better to move forward slowly and consistently than to take giant steps sporadically, especially if the changes don't last. Change gets more difficult as we get older. Remember:

1. The earlier in life we become observant, the more time we have to accumulate *mitzvahs*.

2. If we miss an opportunity to move forward, it may not come our way again.

3. Going forward slowly still means moving forward.

6. Buy The Special Prayer Book For Each Holiday.

Although the prayers for each holiday are similar to the daily and *Shabbos* prayers in many respects, it will be much easier for you if you buy the special *machzorim* (prayer books) for Rosh Hashanah, Yom Kippur, Selichos, Tishah B'Av, Sukkos, Pesach and Shavuous. In addition, if you have the time, it would be helpful to sit down with a rabbi before each holiday and have him walk you through the prayer service, since the customs at any particular *shul* will differ slightly from the layout of the *machzor*.

7. Ask Questions

Somewhere along the way, you will be shocked by something you hear. If you take the time to ask a question, you may find, as I have on many occasions, that your initial understanding is exactly the opposite of what the speaker was trying to convey. If you get lost when you are praying, don't be afraid to ask where everyone else is up to. Your neighbors will be happy to help you.

8. Become Involved In The Observant Community.

Send a check (as little as $18 is usually okay) to some orthodox shuls or organizations and ask to be put on their mailing list. Go to lectures. Eat at kosher restaurants and frequent Jewish bookstores. Go to *Shabbos* services at different synagogues. When people invite you to stay at their home for the entire *Shabbos* or to come for a meal, don't hesitate to accept.

9. Incorporate Hebrew And Yiddish Into Your Everyday Speech

Many observant Jews sprinkle their conversation with Hebrew and Yiddish. Not because they can't speak perfect

English, but because historically, our language has been one of the primary ways in which we have identified ourselves as Jews. Two terms that come to mind are *im yirtza Hashem* (G-d willing) and *Baruch Hashem* (thank G-d).

10. Take Your Religious Commitment Seriously, Not Yourself

I am the first to admit that taking on *mitzvahs* is difficult. So when I see someone who is not observing them in the manner I was taught, I can get a little frustrated. The question I have to ask myself is, "Am I upset because I somehow believe that person has done something to me (i.e. my ego), or is it because they have done something to desecrate *Hashem*'s name?" In fact, it is almost always the former.

Ten More Practical Tips

1. Become Familiar With Recent Jewish Heroes

Some incredible Jews have lived in the last two centuries. Take the time to learn about them; you will draw strength from their example. ArtScroll/Mesorah Publications and C.I.S. Publishers each has an entire series on Jewish heroes. Check them out.

2. Attend A Yeshiva (Men) Or Seminary (Women)

For a couple of weeks, or a couple of years. There is nothing that can replace the intense learning that a *yeshiva/ seminary* environment provides. I was lucky that one of the greatest *yeshivas* in the world (Telshe) was located practically in my backyard. I moved to within walking distance of the yeshiva study hall for about one year. It was one of the best decisions I have ever made. Although I wasn't formally enrolled, I probably learned more about the incredible benefits of living as an observant Jew—almost by happenstance—just by living in the Telshe community, than I would have learned by going to classes.

3. Stay Close To Your Family

We expect our families to immediately share our newfound excitement about our religious observance. Don't. They are about as interested in religion as you were before you started learning. When I was becoming observant, I thought that I would transform my family with my logic and exuberance. What I learned was:

Don't expect your family to accept the new you right away. If you are planning on making a change (i.e. taking on a new *mitzvah*), give your family as much time as possible to get used to the idea.

Don't be confrontational. If one of them says something that denigrates your new commitment, respond with a question, not an accusation.

Grandchildren solve most problems. Enough said.

4. Watch Less TV

For many years, it seemed as if the remote control was part of my hand. For over a year I tried to watch less TV. My game plan was to first give up the premium cable channels like HBO and Showtime, then give up all the cable channels, and finally, give up watching TV altogether. No matter how hard I tried, though, I just couldn't make that first call to the cable company. I ended up going cold turkey and not bringing my TV's with me when I moved to a new apartment. As with most *mitzvahs*, I had a lot more anxiety thinking about it than actually doing it.

5. Learn Some Hebrew Songs

At first it might seem strange, but one of the great joys of *Shabbos* is being able to join in the singing. Joy is an integral part of being Jewish, and singing helps ferment that joy.

6. Get A Hebrew Calender

There is a wealth of information in Hebrew calendars. You are going to be observing many new holidays, along with *Rosh Chodesh*—the beginning of each Jewish month. It's best to know in advance when they will fall out. Did you ever wonder why in certain years the Jewish holidays "come late?" It's because the Jewish calendar has leap years, when we insert an entire extra month into the calendar.

7. Don't Judge The Torah By Individuals You Perceive As Torah Observant

No one is perfect. Everybody has shortcomings. Observant Jews have shortcomings *in spite* of being observant, not because of their observance.

8. Learn The Hebrew You Need To Avoid Embarrassment

Basic Blessings. The blessings which we say before and after eating any type of food can be found in most prayer books and *benchers* (books containing the Grace after Meals).

Aliyahs. When a man is called up to the Torah, he must recite an introduction and two short blessings before the Torah is read, plus one after. When you are called, you may want to take your prayer book with you, even if they have the blessings on a sheet of paper on the *bima* (the elevated table on which the Torah is placed), because you will be more familiar with the format, and the Torah sometimes covers the paper on the *bima*.

Benching—Grace after Meals. After eating bread, we recite Grace after Meals. If there are three men over the age of 13 present, an adult male is designated as the "leader." The leader must recite certain introductory statements out loud, plus the last sentence of four of the paragraphs. Learn the leader's part, because when you go to someone's house for *Shabbos*, you will undoubtedly be given the honor of leading the *benching*. In addition, there is a blessing that guests say for their hosts immediately after reciting the *benching*. Try to learn that as well.

Responses During Prayer. During each *kaddish*, the congregation says aloud, "Amen. May His great name be blessed forever and ever." Learn how to pronounce this correctly (in Hebrew) and when to say it. There are other responses, including "Blessed is He," which you should also learn.

9. Take Advantage Of The Chazzan's Repetition Of The Silent Amidah

Don't waste the precious moments that *Hashem* sets aside every day to listen to your requests. If you finish the *Amidah* before the *chazzan* has finished his repetition, take that time to thank *Hashem* for everything you have. Pray for the health and welfare of your family and friends. Take a moment to pray for the intelligence to complete a business transaction, or to understand a page of *Gemara*. Pray for a *rebbe*. Pray for the strength to withstand difficult challenges. Pray to be forgiven for committing a wrongdoing. Pray for the coming of *Mashiach* (Messiah). Don't be shy.

10. Make Yourself A Rebbe

I can't emphasize this point enough.

Your Story

My story in not unique, by any means. I have heard many stories from people like me.

Some relate to how they started to become observant.

Others have to do with their connection to grandparents who had been observant.

Still others revolve around a particular rabbi.

A number of the stories describe the inexplicable ways in which they met their spouse.

And, of course, there are humorous stories that accompany all of our journeys.

Are you willing to share your story with others?

If so, please contact me by sending an e-mail to FF2E@core.com; or send me a note to PO Box, 21647, Cleveland, Ohio, 44121-0647.

All submissions will be confidential. I will submit what I write back to you for your approval. If, after seeing it, you have a change of heart, I will simply hit "delete" on my computer and that will be the end of it.

Glossary

Aliyah. Literally, an "elevation." Also the term for being called to say the *brachas* before the public reading of the *Torah* in *shul*, as in: "He got an *aliyah.*"

Amidah. Basic prayer in which we ask *Hashem* for wisdom, health, forgiveness, financial security, protection and all of our other personal needs, and the needs of mankind in general. It is sometimes called the silent *Amidah* because it is said quietly.

Avairah. Literally it means "missing the mark." A sin, but not in the secular sense.

Ba'al teshuva. Literally, "one who has returned." Someone who has returned to an observant lifestyle.

Baruch Hashem. Thank G-d.

Bashert. The person who Hashem decided is perfectly suited for you to marry. Also, "pre-ordained," as in: "It was *bashert* that I ran into Shimon because he told me about that stock when it was only $4 per share."

Bimah. Platform onto which the Torah is placed for reading.

Bris. Circumcision performed according to *halacha.*

Bircas hamazon (benching). Blessing said after eating bread.

Bochur. An unmarried male student.

Brachah. A blessing.

Chasunah. A wedding.

Chavrusa. A study partner.

Chometz. Literally, something that is "leavened" or has "risen". Many products, including bread, pasta, cookies, crackers, cereals, and many more items are *chometz,* and cannot be eaten on Pesach.

Chumash. The Five Books of Moses: Genesis, Exodus, Leviticus, Numbers, and Deuteronomy.

Daven. To pray.

Erev. Just prior to. As in *erev Shabbos.*

Frum. Someone who observes *mitzvahs.*

FFB. (Frum from birth). Jews who have been observant/ *frum* their entire lives.

Halacha. Jewish law.

Hamotzi. Blessing which is said before eating bread.

Gemara. The commentary on the earliest codification of Jewish oral law.

Gut Voch. Literally, "Good week." Traditional greeting said the evening after *Shabbos.*

Hashem. Literally, "The Name." G-d.

Hechsherim. The symbols that designate a product as kosher which appear on the labels of most kosher foods.

Im yirtza Hashem. G-d willing.

Kaballah. Literally, "The Hidden Torah," but more popularly known as Jewish mysticism.

Kasher. To make something kosher.

Kashrut. As in, the "laws of *Kashrut.*"

Kavana. Intent.

Kiddush. Prayer inaugurating *Shabbos* and holidays, said over a cup of wine.

Klal Yisroel. The Jewish people.

Kiruv. Outreach. Usually with respect to organizations that work with Jews who are not *FFB's.*

Mensch. Literally, a "man" in Yiddish, but more generally, a person of good character.

Mitzrayim. Egypt.

Kibud av v'aim. Literally, to "honor your father and mother."

Kohein. Literally, a "priest." A descendent of Aharon, the brother of Moshe.

Kollel. A center of study for young married post-graduate Torah students,

Loshon hora. Gossip, slander.

Mezuzahs. Literally, a "doorpost." The parchment scroll inscribed with the *Shema* (not the ornamental cover), which is affixed to doorposts.

Mikvah. A ritual bath.

Minyan. A quorum of at least ten men over the age of 13.

Mishna. The earliest codification of Jewish oral law.

Mitzvah. A commandment to act or refrain from an act.

Neshama. A soul.

Parsha. A chapter in the *Chumash.*

Payos. Sideburns.

Posuk. A sentence.

Rebbe. Too difficult to define in a Glossary. See Step 2, "Make Yourself A Rebbe."

Rebbetzin. The wife of a rabbi.

Rosh. Head or leader.

Seder. The evening meal on the first two nights of Passover.

Sefer. A book.

Segula. A special sign.

Shabbos. The Sabbath. From Friday night to Saturday night.

Shacharis. Literally, "morning," but usually refers to the full complement of morning prayers.

Shaatnez. A mixture of wool and linen.

Shidduch. The process by which you meet your marriage partner or the person you will marry.

Siddur. Prayer book.

Shiur. A class, usually related to a Torah subject.

Shomer. Literally a "watchman." Someone who watches or keeps a *mitzvah,* as in "being *shomer Shabbos.*"

Shul. A synagogue.

Simcha. Literally "joy," but often related to an event, as in, "Are you going to the *simcha?*"

Tallis. A prayer shawl with *tzitzis* at each corner used during *davening.*

Talmid. Student.

Tefillin. Two black leather boxes containing verses from the Torah which describe the unique bond of love between *Hashem* and the Jewish people. They are bound to the head and arm of adult males during morning prayers.

Toivelling. Immersing certain pots, pans, dishes, silverware and other utensils in the *mikvah.*

Tzaddik. A righteous man.

Tzaddekes. A righteous women.

Tzeddakah. Charity.

Torah. Literally, "instructions." The Five Books of Moses, the Prophets and the Oral Law.

Tzitzis. Literally, "fringes." A four-cornered garment with fringes attached to each corner that are collectively tied into 613 knots to remind us of the 613 *mitzvahs.*

Yeshiva. A high school/college for Jewish students.

Yidden. Jews.

Yom Tov. Holiday.